HUMOR
WORKS

John Morreall, Ph.D.

HRD Press, Inc.
Amherst, Massachusetts

D1041300

ISBN 0-87425-400-0

Published by: **HRD Press, Inc.**
      22 Amherst Road
      Amherst, MA 01002
      800 822-2801
      (413) 253-3490 (FAX)
      Internet: http://www.hrdpress.com

Production and Graphics by *Page Design Services*
Editorial Services by Lisa Wood
Cover Design by Eileen Klockars

For Tamara, my partner in the funny business of life.

Table of Contents

PREFACE

In the last ten years there has been an explosion of interest in humor. Half of the current trade paperback bestsellers are books of cartoons. Situation comedies dominate network television. One cable TV channel broadcasts nothing but humor. Most cities have at least one comedy club, and standup comedians now number in the thousands.

Along with this desire to enjoy humor, there is a growing interest in its benefits. The Humor Project's Tenth Annual International Conference on the Positive Power of Humor and Creativity recently drew over a thousand participants. Medical researchers are investigating how laughter stimulates the immune system. Over 30,000 nurses subscribe to the *Journal of Nursing Jocularity*. Hundreds of businesses are holding seminars on how humor reduces stress and promotes teamwork.

When I started to write this book, there were already dozens of books about the benefits of humor. Why, then, add another? My background, I need to confess, is academic. My earlier books are on the philosophy of humor, and for years I've taught courses on humor and comedy. As I read the books on the benefits of humor, I found jokes, funny stories, and tips. But I didn't find clear answers to basic questions: *What* is humor? *How* does it reduce stress? *Why* is it so closely related to creativity? It may be an academic prejudice, but I wanted a book that had not only funny material and tips, but *explanations*. There was no such book, so I wrote this one.

If I started thanking my colleagues in management, psychology, and other areas who have given me good ideas, there would be no fair place to stop. So let me simply acknowledge the inspiration of two trailblazers. The first is the pioneer of contemporary humor studies, Dr. William F. Fry, Jr., emeritus associate clinical professor of psychiatry at Stanford University, whose 1963 *Sweet Madness* and subsequent research cleared a path for people like me to follow. And the second is Dr. Joel Goodman, who pioneered the field of humor training with his Humor Project in Saratoga Springs, New York, and his journal, *Laughing Matters*. All of us who study humor or train people in its value owe these gentlemen a great deal.

I also want to thank the thousands of people in my Humorworks Seminars over the last several years. They have asked great questions, have shown me how to make my ideas clear, and have told wonderful stories, many of which appear in this book.

CHAPTER 1

PLAY IS NOT THE OPPOSITE OF WORK

The Traditional Prejudice against Humor and Play

Sometimes when I tell people that I do seminars on humor in the workplace, they look at me as if I had said I manufacture square wheels. As one woman said to me recently, "Humor and work—you've got to be kidding!" In her mind I had contradicted myself. Humor is a kind of play, and she knew—or thought she knew—that play is the opposite of work. When we laugh or do something that's fun in my seminars, I sometimes notice a guilty look on certain faces. These people don't say what they are feeling, but if they did, it would be, "I'm on the clock, so I shouldn't be laughing or enjoying myself."

This attitude has a long history. American culture was founded by Puritans and others who lived by the work ethic. They believed that hard work is what life is all about, that the solution to any problem is to work harder, and that work requires a solemn "nose to the grindstone" attitude. Our work ethic is part of the more ancient warrior philosophy, in which life is thought of as a series of battles, and we fight our way through life with a tough, narrowly focused, no-nonsense attitude. The good person has the virtues of a good soldier: discipline, unquestioning obedience to authority, and full concentration on one task at a time.

In the work ethic and the warrior philosophy the only acceptable emotions are tough "masculine" emotions, such as anger, that energize us to overcome enemies and obstacles. Joy, compassion, amusement, and other positive experiences are out. So are non-practical kinds of thinking requiring imagination and critical thinking. Anything that smacks of play—doing something because it's fun—is automatically suspect. Because of these philosophies, even workers' morale was not a concern of management until late in this century. In the 1922 edition of *The Management Handbook*, one page out of 2,281 was devoted to the subject of morale.

The traditional attitude toward laughter and play was spelled out clearly in the rules of a church school in colonial America:

> We prohibit play in the strongest terms.
> The student shall rise at five in the morning,
> summer and winter. And the student shall be
> indulged in nothing which the world calls
> play. Let this rule be observed with strictest
> nicety, for those who play when they are
> young will play when they are old.

But this prejudice is much older than our country. It was already well-established in the Bible and ancient Greece. The book of Ecclesiastes warned that "The fool lifts up his voice with laughter, but the wise man scarcely smiles a little." The Greek philosopher Plato thought that in an ideal society, comedy and laughter would be eliminated. His student Aristotle did not want to outlaw humor and play, but he saw play as valuable only because it refreshed us for more work. We play, he said, because we cannot work all the time.

In the Middle Ages many orders of monks had rules against laughter and play. When the Puritans came to political power in England in the seventeenth century, they outlawed comedy and stage plays altogether. And in the following centuries up to our own, there were many condemnations of laughter. "There is nothing more unbecoming a man of quality," wrote William Congreve, "than to laugh." Joseph Addison attacked laughter because it "slackens and unbraces the mind, weakens the faculties, and causes a kind of remissness and dissolution in all the powers of the soul." The diplomat and writer Lord Chesterfield had this comment in a letter to his son:

> Having mentioned laughing, I must particularly warn you against it. Frequent and loud laughter is the characteristic of folly and ill manners. . . . I am neither of a melancholy nor a cynical disposition, but I am sure that since I had full use of my reason, nobody has heard me laugh.

In the early 1800s the poet Shelley wrote, "I am convinced that there can be no entire regeneration of mankind until laughter is put down." The Victorian era saw whole books condemning laughter, such as George Vasey's *A Philosophy of Laughter and Smiling*. Laughter makes our faces twisted and ugly, according to Vasey, and it disrupts our normal heartbeat and breathing—he cites cases of people who laughed to death. Indeed, for Vasey laughter was a dangerous and wholly unnatural habit comparable to masturbation, considered by Victorians one of the most dangerous vices. If babies were treated rationally, Vasey wrote, they would never laugh at all. But instead we pick them up; toss, jostle, and tickle them; and blow on their tummies to make rude noises, all of which forces them into the nervous spasms we call laughter. Then they grow up and pass laughter on to their children. If we would only stop this nasty practice for one generation, Vasey wrote, laughter would die out and perhaps we could reverse the decline of the human race.

In our own century there have been many similar attacks on laughter and humor. In *The Secret of Laughter* Anthony Ludovici described humor as a way of ducking responsibilities: the noble, hard-working person would never laugh.

> Humor is, therefore, the lazier principle to adopt in approaching all questions, and that is why the muddle is increasing everywhere. Because the humorous mind shirks the heavy task of solving thorny problems and prefers to make people laugh about them ... Truth to tell, there is in every inspired and passionate innovator a haughty energy which is incompatible with the cowardice and indolence of humor.[1]

It's not necessary to pile up more of these condemnations of laughter and play. The general idea is clear. According to the Puritan work ethic, life consists of achieving goals. But laughter and play don't accomplish anything. The only possible justification for such useless activities, then, would be if they refresh us for more work, or if they can be turned into goal-oriented activities.

One way our culture has found to make play into goal-oriented activity is games, preferably games modeled on war, like football and hockey. Play becomes acceptable, that is, when its playfulness is eliminated and it is turned into another form of work. True play—doing something for the fun of it—would be frivolous, foolish, and silly. We give children this message when we encourage them to "work hard" at practicing their athletic skills and we give them pep talks about "No pain, no gain." Then when they win the Little League game, say, we praise them with "Good *work*. You did a good *job*." Many parents get upset when their children lose. In their minds, being in a game is working toward a victory, and so losing is failing at one's work. Next time, they tell their kids, you'll work harder and you'll win.

In a culture based on the Puritan work ethic, the only people exempt from the ban on non-goal-directed activity are those like preschoolers who cannot even engage in sports. For a few years they are allowed to simply play. We warn them, however, that this time will be brief, and they should not get attached to play, for playing is frivolous and foolish. One popular piece of propaganda here is the Golden Books version of Walt Disney's *Three Little Pigs*. In case you haven't put a three-year-old to bed recently, let's recall the story.

"Once upon a time there were three little pigs who went out into the big world to build their homes and seek their fortunes. The first little pig did not like to work at all. He quickly built himself a house of straw. Then off he danced down the road, to see how his brothers were

5

getting along." As he dances he plays a flute and his hat is bobbing off his head.

The second little pig is also a lazy musician. "He did not like to work any better than his brother, so he had decided to build a quick and easy house of sticks. . . . It was not a very strong little house, but at least the work was done." Now these two danced down the road, to the tune of their fiddle and flute, to see how their brother was doing.

"The third little pig was a sober little pig. He was building a house, too, but he was building his of bricks. He did not mind hard work, and he wanted a stout little, strong little house, for he knew that in the woods nearby there lived a big bad wolf who liked nothing better than to catch little pigs and eat them up!" In the Disney cartoon, this pig's name is "Practical" and his joyless "nose to the grindstone" attitude ends up saving his lazy brothers' lives. The contrast between his hard-working humorlessness and their lazy laughter is made again and again. "'Ha ha ha!' laughed the first little pig, when he saw his brother hard at work. 'Ho ho ho!' laughed the second little pig. 'Come down and play with us!' he called. But the busy little pig did not even pause. Slap, slosh, slap! went bricks on mortar as he called down to them:

> "'I build my house of stones.
> I build my house of bricks.
> I have no chance
> To sing and dance,
> For work and play don't mix.'"

Again the two lazy pigs laugh at their sensible brother. "You can laugh and dance and sing," he calls after them, "but I'll be safe and you'll be sorry when the wolf comes to the door." And just to make sure that even the youngest child understands how foolish the first two pigs are, the book has them laugh at their brother yet again and disappear into the woods singing "Who's Afraid of the Big Bad Wolf?" immediately after which the wolf pops out of the woods to attack them.

The message here is obvious: we can have a good time, can laugh and dance and sing, but if we do, we are lazy jerks who can't provide for even our basic needs like shelter and safety. To be good people, we need to be like Practical Pig—humorless, joyless workaholics.

When kids begin school, they are bombarded with the idea that life is a series of tasks, and that laughter and fun only get in the way of accomplishing anything. How many times are kids scolded with lines like "Grow up—get serious" and "Wipe that stupid grin off your face"? They are in school to "do their work," we tell them, and at home they do their homework, so that they can move through the educational mill, get jobs, and work for another forty or fifty years.

Play is sometimes permitted at school, but only as relaxation before going back to work, and then only under a set of rules to keep everything under control. Humor is generally viewed as not controllable in school, and so is suppressed. Indeed, it is not encouraged even for preschool kids. As one study of Head Start classrooms showed, teachers who are supervising *play* often discourage four-year-olds from laughing or being funny!

I can still remember my first week of first grade and my teacher's voice booming out "What's so *funny,* Mr. Morreall?" Not knowing any better, I answered with a smile, "My lunch bag fell behind the radiator." Not only was she not amused, but she was upset at my answering her question instead of being humiliated and silenced by it. Indeed, a lot of teachers even today consider "What's so *funny,* Mr./Miss _____?" one of their most successful put-downs. The assumption, of course, is that if students find anything funny in school, there is something wrong with them, or at least their desire to work. They should suppress their perverse urge to laugh, and get back to work. While kids who show a talent for music may be sent to the music room, and kids with an artistic bent may be sent to the art room, kids who show a sense of humor are sent to the vice-principal's office.

By the time they are in second or third grade, most kids on the success-track have absorbed the work ethic, think like the Third Little Pig, and stifle their laughter and playfulness. Those who do not, have trouble in school. By third grade, for example, Thomas Edison had been branded "unteachable." For those who do well in school, life becomes a series of tasks, or as the old saying goes, one damned thing after another.

And so curious, imaginative, joyful children sometimes grow into the joyless adults we see all around us. Kids who at age five had laughed hundreds of times a day, become adults who laugh fifteen times a day.

What gets lost here is not just laughter. We also lose emotional range. As C.W. Metcalf and Roma Felible point out in their book *Lighten Up*, while as four-year-olds most of us had over a dozen facial expressions, many of us now have just two or three. If we are really successful, we may go through the rest of life with just one face, the mask of professional cool, which accompanies both "Ms. Crawford, is it too late to reschedule my flight?" and "You're leaving me, Katherine? Why would you do something like that?"[2]

The philosophy of the Third Little Pig never made anybody particularly fulfilled or happy, but at least it seemed useful in building America into an industrial nation. People came to work, punched the clock, did what they were told for eight or ten hours, and our industrial economy grew. When a problem came up, working harder and longer would usually solve it.

But now we are in a postindustrial economy. Seventy-nine percent of U.S. workers are officially classified as in the service sector, and even among the 19 percent of us counted as in manufacturing, 90 percent are involved in services—design, engineering, sales, etc. So a whopping 96 percent of the American workforce are in services.[3] In the service sector and even in manufacturing, it's no longer enough that people show up for work and follow simple instructions. Simply working harder and longer doesn't solve our small-scale problems today, much less our national problems. Twenty-five years ago the U.S. was the world's largest exporter and the largest creditor nation. Today, with many more people working, and working harder and longer, we are the world's largest importer and the largest debtor nation.

The work ethic no longer works. In fact it suppresses many of the traits needed in our hi-tech postindustrial workplace. We now want people who are enthusiastic and willing to take risks; who can think on their feet, see things from several perspectives, and come up with creative solutions to problems. We want people who are socially versatile, too; who can create rapport, motivate others, and work smoothly in teams. In short, we want people who can see their work as challenging, socially satisfying, and fun. But these are precisely the traits that the Puritan work ethic takes out of workers.

The traditional American workplace was run by principles laid down early in this century by Frederick W. Taylor in books such as *Scientific Management*. Under Taylorism workers were assumed to be lazy and untrustworthy, and so were kept isolated from one other as much as possible. Large jobs requiring skill and judgment were divided into small jobs requiring no skill or decision-making. Thinking and dealing with people were management functions. This system made it easy and cheap to train and replace workers. But it also asked them to leave their brains, their enthusiasm, and their social skills at home. Industrial work was the repetition of small mindless tasks from which all traces of challenge and fun had been removed.

As we have moved into a postindustrial economy, we require more of people than a few mindless tasks repeated until retirement. And so we need to replace the outmoded philosophies of Taylorism and the Puritan work ethic, to allow people not only to live more meaningful lives, but to do better work!

To test your own confidence, or lack of confidence, in the work ethic, ask yourself a few questions. Have you ever seen a stupid, unimaginative standup comic? Why do great inventors, and people in creative fields like advertising, typically have above-average senses of humor? Who in your workplace shows the best sense of humor and the most playful attitude toward work? Isn't it the clever, innovative, creative people?

Is play really the opposite of seriousness? Take a look at a child playing, or at an artist, musician, or athlete. Are they serious about what they are doing? You bet. But they are playing, too. The highest activities of human beings and some of their greatest accomplishments, in fact, are play. Indeed, when religious people have tried to picture what heaven might be like, they have pictured it as a kind of play. The philosopher John Dewey got it right: "To be playful and serious at the same time is possible, and it defines the ideal mental condition."

Even when we have a specific practical goal to accomplish, a playful attitude can help. Think of the projects on which you have worked that came out the best. Were they "nose to the grindstone" drudgery, or were they projects that challenged you mentally, involved interesting interactions with other people, and were in other ways fun?

Where creative thinking and problem-solving are a big part of the work, wise managers are careful to encourage a spirit of fun. As David Ogilvy, head of a major advertising agency, put it, "When people aren't having any fun, they seldom produce good advertising. Kill grimness with laughter. Maintain an atmosphere of informality. Encourage exuberance."[4]

A classic example of the connection between fun, creativity, and productivity was the inventor Thomas Edison, who had 1,093 patents, among them patents for the light bulb, the phonograph, and the movie projector.

Near the end of his long and productive career, Edison had this comment: "I never did a day's work in my life—it was all fun!" Edison was kidding, of course; he was lampooning the traditional prejudice against fun as counterproductive. His idea was simply that the best work—the most satisfying work and the most productive work—*is* fun.

Edison's sense of humor and fun could be seen in everything he did. His notebooks contained many funny sketches and sayings, and after his death one of the drawers in his desk was found to hold slips of paper with humorous quotations on them. Even his inventions revealed his sense of humor. As a young man he worked in a filthy, vermin-infested shop which the owner refused to clean up. One morning Edison hooked up some electrodes to the top of his workbench that instantly electrocuted any cockroach walking onto the bench. Soon everyone in the shop was waiting for the crackling sound and distinctive odor of the next electrocuted roach, and laughing and cheering when it happened. Edison's device had made the vermin problem graphic, public, and funny. By the end of the day the owner agreed to clean up the shop.

And you don't have to be an Edison to benefit from bringing your sense of humor and fun to work. Humor is valuable for everyone. Compared to people who don't find fun in their work, people who do report that they are less anxious and depressed, more satisfied with their jobs and with their lives generally, more motivated by their work, more creative at doing it, better able to meet job demands, and less likely to be absent or late for work.[5]

The New Appreciation of Humor and Play in the Workplace

Fortunately, in the last decade, enlightened managers have started to appreciate the values of humor, play, and fun. Business publications like *Fortune*, *Forbes*, *Business Week*, *The Nation's Business*, and the *Wall Street Journal* have featured many articles on the benefits of humor. Tom Peters, one of the most respected business consultants in America, has long touted the importance of humor for its fostering of team spirit, creativity, and a constructive attitude toward mistakes. In the photo on the back cover of *The Tom Peters Seminar: Crazy Times Call for Crazy Organizations*, his upper torso appears in a coat and tie, and his bottom half in nothing but loud boxer shorts. In *The Pursuit of Wow*, which has Peters juggling on the cover, he recommends this philosophy: "Have a collegial, supportive, yeasty, zany, laughter-filled environment where folks support one another."[6]

One CEO who has made a name for himself, and his company, with his sense of humor, is Herb Kelleher of Southwest Airlines. The cover story of the May 4, 1994 *Fortune* asks, "Is Herb Kelleher America's Best CEO? He's wild, he's crazy, he's in a tough business—and he has built the most successful airline in the U.S." The cover photo shows Kelleher in a WWI-style leather aviator's helmet and goggles, flying with only his arms. The story shows how Kelleher's humor, business savvy, and ability to create team spirit are interrelated. In hiring people, Kelleher says, "what we are looking for, first and foremost, is a sense of humor. ...We don't care that much about education and expertise, because we can train people. ...We hire attitudes." One of the attitudes Kelleher is looking for, he calls "an insouciance, an effervescence." Right in the job interview, in fact, prospective employees are asked, "Tell me how you recently used your sense of humor in a work environment. Tell me how you have used humor to defuse a difficult situation."

Southwest workers are encouraged to amuse, surprise and entertain passengers. During delays at the gate, for example, ticket agents will award prizes to the passengers with the most unusual items in their pockets or purses. Safety announcements at the beginning of a flight may begin: "There are fifty ways to leave your lover, but only six exits from this airplane." A few years ago the Federal Aviation Administration asked Southwest to stop *singing* the safety announcements to the tune of the *Beverly Hillbillies* theme song. The fun atmosphere created by this humor is part of the high level of service that puts Southwest at the top of customer service polls.

This atmosphere is also important to employees, who often speak of Southwest as a family, something rarely said about other airlines, or other corporations, these days. Alan Boyd, retired chairman of Airbus North America, commented that "at other places, managers say that people are their most important resource, but nobody acts on it. At Southwest, they have never lost sight of the fact."

It's no wonder that Southwest Airlines was rated in the top ten places to work in the book *The Hundred Best Companies to Work for in America.*[7] The authors of that book cite companies' attitudes toward playfulness and fun as something people mention often in praising or criticizing their workplace. Indeed, the book puts Southwest Airlines on a list of six companies "WHERE FUN IS

A WAY OF LIFE." "Today, fun is not inconsistent with operating a serious business," the authors comment. "Watch out for companies where there is no sense of humor."[8]

In a survey of vice presidents and personnel directors of one hundred large corporations, 84 percent said that employees with a sense of humor do a better job. According to Robert Half, who conducted the survey, that's because "people with a sense of humor tend to be more creative, less rigid, and more willing to consider and embrace new ideas and methods."[9] In another study done in 1985 by Richard Cronin, head of an executive search firm, questionnaires were sent to the Fortune 500 CEOs and to deans of leading business schools. Of the more than 300 CEOs who replied, over 97 percent agreed that humor is important to the conduct of business, that executives should develop a greater sense of humor, and that in a hiring decision, they give preference to the candidate with the best sense of humor.

Most of the CEOs also had a culprit to blame for what they saw as the decline of humor in business—it was the narrowly focused MBA programs, whose graduates now dominate major corporations. As you might expect, only half of the business school deans agreed that humor is declining in business, although more agreed that the narrow technical disciplines taught in their schools are largely to blame for the great number of "cheerless corporate managers" who treat humor as a waste of time.

I'm happy to report an encouraging new sign from one MBA program, the prestigious Wharton Business School. A student of mine recently applied there and asked me to write an evaluation letter for him. Among the characteristics the form asked me to comment on was "the candidate's sense of humor."

To incorporate humor into the workplace, many companies have hired humor consultants. John Cleese, from *Monty Python's Flying Circus* and other TV and film comedy, has become the world's largest producer of training films largely through the skillful use of humor in his 120 training films.

Humor has even gone hi-tech. "The Humor Processor" from Responsive Software contains an indexed database of jokes and a brainstorming section for generating original humor—"over 100,000 comedic combinations," according to the ads. For business speakers there's WordStar International's software "Just Joking," with over 2,800 jokes and humorous quotations under more than 250 topics. The computer disks even come with a pair of Groucho glasses with the big nose and hairy eyebrows.

Some of the companies who are incorporating humor and playfulness into the workplace are small and entrepreneurial. Dreyer's Grand Ice Cream goes so far as to have a policy that people cannot become supervisors unless they can create fun and arouse enthusiasm in other people. Ben and Jerry's Ice Cream has a Joy Committee with the motto: "If it's not fun, we don't want to do it." Activities include a Tacky Dress-Up Day and hired masseuses during times of extra tension. Explained Peter Lind, head of research and development, and Grand Poobah of the Joy Committee, this relaxed attitude is part of Ben and Jerry's whole approach to management, in which people can relax with each other and so be more productive. "There's not a hierarchy here. People can share ideas," Lind said in an article aptly titled "All Work and No Play Isn't Even Good for Work."[10]

But ice cream companies aren't the only ones who have institutionalized humor and play. Many hi-tech electronics companies are famous for their fun atmosphere. Odetics, a robotics firm in Anaheim, California, has had a Fun Committee for over ten years, sponsoring events like 50s and 60s Days, with telephone-booth stuffing and Hula-Hoop and bubble-blowing contests. They also have fun with their products. One group built ODEX, a six-legged robot that roams the hallways like a giant spider. Their attitude also shows in the weight room, pool, tennis and volleyball courts, and the repertory theater Odetics provides for use by everyone in the company. As Bill Pritchard, manager of public relations and member of the Fun Committee, explains, facilities like these improve communication and morale. In the fitness center, everyone from the maintenance staff to the president can be found exercising, and that promotes an openness and good feeling throughout the company.

Even respected older corporations have gotten the message. Eastman Kodak, Price-Waterhouse, Hewlett-Packard, and Digital Equipment have designed special rooms for their employees as humor rooms, play rooms, or creativity rooms. Hewlett-Packard's is painted in bright primary colors like a preschool. Kodak's twenty-by-fifty-foot humor room is stocked with Monty Python and Candid Camera videos, Dave Barry and Erma Bombeck books, and props to help employees lighten up. It has four main sections: a publications and media resource center; a computer area with software employees can use to write jokes and stimulate their creativity; a presentation area with AV equipment; and a "Toy Store" with props and gags, costumes, and juggling supplies. The creator of Kodak's humor room, industrial engineer Lindsay Collier, said that he'd like to change the traditional attitude that fun and work are contradictory to the point where Kodak workers put up signs saying, "Thank God it's Monday."

At one of its plants, Digital Equipment has even created a "Grouch Patrol." Patrol members who spot someone looking surly make a bat face at the person. This is a useful maneuver in lots of situations, so why not practice it right now? Extend one arm in back of your head and then bring your hand forward across the top of your head. With two fingers pull your nostrils up until they are flared like a bat's. Now flick your tongue in and out rapidly, making a high-pitched "eeeeee" sound. (If you need more detailed instructions, see the book *Lighten Up*, pages 54-59.) Of course, the person who has a bat face made at them still has the choice to remain grouchy, but it's hard. When someone has gone to that much trouble, and has looked that silly, just to get you out of your bad mood, it's hard not to respond positively.

Even Wall Street has a secret society—the Underwear Underground—a group of stockbrokers who wear Mickey Mouse underwear to work each Friday.

Now much of this humor is simply comic relief from stressful work, temporary withdrawal from whatever is going on. And that provides a valuable kind of refreshment. But if humor stops with comic relief, we've missed its deeper value, which is found not outside, but within work itself. If humor were just a momentary distraction, a toy, it *would be* trivial, as many people have charged. But thinking of humor as mere recreation is like thinking of oil paintings as a nice way to cover up cracks in the walls.

In this book we will not spend much time on the type humor that is merely a distraction or a toy. We will be looking at a deeper kind of humor that empowers us *in* our work, rather than distracting us *from* our work. I see an analogy here between humor and the wheel. Before Europeans came to the Americas, the native people had invented the wheel, but they used it only on toys. They had not made the next step of using it on real vehicles. I'm convinced that if people stopped thinking of humor as a toy, and started seeing its usefulness within work situations themselves, they would find themselves with something every bit as wonderful as the wheel.

Let me close this chapter with an example of the kind of humor I have in mind. It comes from a Xerox research department a few years ago, known to insiders as the "Skunk Works" (a name taken from Al Capp's "L'il Abner" comic strip). Housed in a dilapidated building in East Rochester, New York, the department specified in its lease that no improvements were to be made to the inside of the building. Sections of wallboard were broken away from exposed studs, and in spots visitors walked carefully to avoid falling through holes in the floor. Few of the workers wore ties, many wore jeans. "We do drawings on the floor and on the walls," said Skunk Works manager S. William Volkers. "Our best meetings are held in the hallways."

The run-down look of the place gave it the informal, egalitarian atmosphere of a garage workshop, which the researchers found liberating and stimulating. The spirit of the Skunk Works was that of a small entrepreneurial venture—and it drew the same kind of enthusiastic dedication from the workers. Its experimental, irreverent, and anti-bureaucratic attitude was expressed in large part through humor. In the employee lounge was a ripped black tie nailed to the wall, and an executive doll in a suit hanged with a little rope. Such rebelliousness would not be tolerated in a traditional business setting, of course, but for the Skunk Works, it was just right for promoting openness, creative thinking, and team spirit. Working on projects with names like "Bulldog" and "Chainsaw," Skunk Works researchers have modified old products, and developed new ones much faster than traditional research departments. Their creativity and speed have saved Xerox millions of dollars.

Places like the Skunk Works show that the Third Little Pig was wrong: work and play do mix.

Notes

1 Ludovici, Anthony, *The Secret of Laughter* (New York: Viking, 1933), pp. 11-13.

2 C.W. Metcalf and Roma Felible, *Lighten Up: Survival Skills for People under Pressure* (New York: Addison-Wesley, 1992), pp. 54-59.

3 Tom Peters, *The Pursuit of Wow! Every Person's Guide to Topsy-Turvy Times* (New York: Vintage, 1994), p. 67.

4 Tom Peters and Robert Waterman, *In Search of Excellence* (New York: Harper & Row, 1982), p. 291.

5 David Abramis, "All Work and No Play Isn't Even Good for Work," *Psychology Today*, March 1989, p. 38.

6 Tom Peters, *The Pursuit of Wow!* (New York: Vintage, 1994), p. 18.

7 Robert Levering and Milton Moscowitz, *The Hundred Best Companies to Work for in America*, 2nd ed. (New York: Doubleday/Currency, 1993).

8 Robert Levering and Milton Moscowitz, "The Workplace 100," *USA Weekend*, January 22-24, 1993, p. 4.

9 Heather Twidale, "Nowadays, Being 'Old Sourpuss' Is No Joke." *Working Woman*, March 1986, p. 18.

10 David Abramis, "All Work and No Play Isn't Even Good for Work," *Psychology Today*, March 1989, pp. 34-38.

CHAPTER 2

MAKING SENSE OF HUMOR

A 2,500-Year-Old Question

T o understand the value of humor, it's good to start with an understanding of what humor is. Since the days of the ancient Greek philosophers, people have argued about the nature of laughter and humor, and the research and discussions are still going strong today. When I teach university courses on humor we review the traditional and modern theories in detail. But for our purposes we can skip the academic debates. If you're interested in theories of laughter and humor, take a look at my book *The Philosophy of Laughter and Humor*, and the first five chapters of my *Taking Laughter Seriously.*[1]

Thinking about humor carefully is difficult because humor takes such different forms. It's hard to see what all funny things might have in common. Is there something shared, for example, by puns, identical twins dressed alike, and spilling your pie on your lap? Most books on humor don't even try to explain what it is, or they skip over the issue with something like, "Humor is what makes us laugh." But it's important to understand what humor is if we want to understand how it works and why it is valuable.

Defining humor simply as "what makes us laugh" is sloppy and confusing, because there is humor that does not make all of us laugh, and there are circumstances that make us laugh—tickling, winning the lottery, seeing a magic trick, and running into an old friend on the street, to name a few—which are not true humor.

Humor is related to laughter, of course, but they are not the same. Laughter is the easier of the two to understand, because, like sneezing or crying, it is something we can watch people do. Humor is a more elusive concept.

The Superiority Theory

The dominant theory of laughter and humor through most of history—from ancient Greece until two hundred years ago—was the Superiority Theory. According to this explanation, laughter is an expression of feelings of superiority over someone else, or over the way we used to be. All laughter is at somebody. Around 1650 the philosopher Thomas Hobbes described laughter as an expression of "sudden glory." Those who laugh the most, he said, are those "who are conscious of the fewest abilities in themselves; who are forced to keep themselves in their own favor by observing the imperfections of other[s]."[2] We might rename this the Don Rickles Theory, in honor of the comedian popular a few years back. Someone who laughs is either, like Don Rickles, humiliating people, or, like someone in Rickles' audience, enjoying seeing people humiliated.

Once we understand that this was the dominant way of thinking about laughter through most of history, it is easier to understand the traditional opposition to laughter and humor. If, whenever I laugh, I am putting someone down, then laughter is essentially nasty and something we should get rid of.

But does the Superiority Theory explain all laughter? Does it give us the essence of laughter or humor? Obviously some cases of laughter and humor involve feelings of superiority, but just as obviously, other cases do not. Babies laugh at "peekaboo," for example, long before they have a sense of themselves to compare with other people. Children and adults sometimes also laugh without feeling superior. When we wake up on an April morning to find snow on the ground, we can laugh out of sheer surprise. And while we sometimes laugh at people's failures and deficiencies, we can also laugh when someone turns out to be *better* than we expected. For example, I once half-heartedly agreed to go to a childen's gymnastic competition, my first, expecting to see a lot of sloppy somersaults and cartwheels. When the first contestant, a seven-year-old girl, did a full back flip from a standing position, I laughed in amazement, but certainly not because I felt superior to her. If anything, I felt inferior. We can also laugh at ourselves when we make a silly mistake, as when we spend five minutes looking for our glasses, only to find them on our head. Obviously, we can't feel superior to the way we are right now, so the laughter here can't be an expression of "sudden glory."

The Incongruity Theory

Feeling better than someone, then, is not the essence of laughter or humor. The Superiority Theory won't do. A more comprehensive explanation of laughter and humor came along two hundred years ago, and now dominates the psychological study of humor. It is called the Incongruity Theory. Like the Superiority Theory, this explanation treats humor as a kind of enjoyment. But according to the Incongruity Theory, what we are enjoying is experiencing something that doesn't fit our mental patterns. Incongruity is a fancy name for a mismatch between what we expect and what we experience. Rough synonyms for "incongruous" are "unexpected," "out-of-place," "strange," "odd," and "abnormal."

If there's a knock at the door and I get up to answer it, for instance, my understanding of the situation is roughly this: there is someone on the other side of the door, and that person wants to talk to me. If my expectations are met, then the situation is normal. But if I open the door and the knocking turns out to be a dog wagging her tail against the door, that's incongruous. And if I enjoy that incongruity, that's humor. Simply put, humor is liking the mental jolt we get when something surprises us. Or more simply, humor is enjoying incongruity.

When I was a college student, a friend of mine put a bowling ball in my refrigerator. The next time I opened the refrigerator, I laughed. There's nothing funny about a refrigerator, and nothing funny about a bowling ball, but putting them together was funny, because my refrigerator was the last place I expected to find a bowling ball.

Not long ago I passed a church with two signs: the one over the door said, "Church of God," and the one on the front lawn, "For Sale by Owner." "He's strapped for cash too?" was my jolting next thought. I enjoyed that mental jolt, so for me the combination of the signs was funny. I'm sure that many people driving by those signs did not relate them and think of God as the owner selling the building, and so for them the signs were not funny. There may also be others who got the same mental picture I got, but did not enjoy it. The signs were not funny to them either. For something to strike us as funny, it has to give us a mental jolt, and we have to enjoy that jolt.

I was shown another sign last year, in the dining room of a retirement home where I was giving a talk. My hostess, who was seventy-six, explained that they were required to post the sign because they occasionally served wine with dinner:

> GOVERNMENT WARNING: ACCORDING TO THE SURGEON GENERAL, WOMEN SHOULD NOT DRINK ALCOHOLIC BEVERAGES DURING PREGNANCY BECAUSE OF THE RISK OF BIRTH DEFECTS.

Now you've seen this sign dozens of times, and it was probably never funny before. In a bar or on a wine bottle the warning makes sense. But in a retirement home, of course, it's pointless and so incongruous.

Another kind of incongruous sign caught my eye recently. I drove to the bank to get some cash. For this simple withdrawal I skipped the drive-up window and drove to the bay with the cash machine. I punched in my secret code and the amount I needed. While waiting for my cash, I looked closely at the slot where I had inserted my bank card and the slot for deposit envelopes. Under each slot was a sign in Braille! As I drove off with my money, I wondered how many blind drivers use that cash machine.

Here's one more sign that was not well thought out, displayed in the window of a jewelry store:

EARS PIERCED WHILE YOU WAIT

Now these signs were all unintentionally funny, but humor in language is usually created intentionally. Most jokes, for example, are designed to lead our minds along one track and then suddenly switch them to a different track. If we enjoy having our train-of-thought switched in this way, then that's humor. In his autobiography, for example, H.L. Mencken wrote, "I never smoked until I was nine." As we read this sentence, everything is going along fine until we get to the last word. Had it been "twenty-nine," that would have been in line with our expectations, and so there would have been no humor. But "nine" is incongruous. It disrupts our mental processing, and if the disruption feels good, that's humor.

A similar jolt occurs in listening to Mae West's comment, "Marriage is a great institution, but I'm not ready for an institution." At the last word we have to shift from our original meaning of "institution" to a quite different one. In jokes generally, the disruption comes at the punch line, as we have to revise our understanding of the first part, or "set-up," of the joke.

As is obvious from my explanation here, to explain humor is to kill it. By spelling out the two meanings of "institution" in the Mae West quip, for example, we soften or eliminate the surprise, and so the incongruity.

We can also see that since humor depends on violating someone's mental patterns in an enjoyable way, nothing is funny all by itself, but only in its ability to have a certain effect on people—to strike them as enjoyably incongruous. Humor is not an objective feature of something, like its color or shape. A hairy green mask with three eyes, for example, isn't automatically funny; it's funny because it's contrary to people's ideas of what faces should look like. On a planet where everyone had three eyes and a hairy green face, that mask wouldn't be funny.

Even on Earth, where hairy green faces with three eyes are incongruous, the mask won't be funny to someone who doesn't enjoy the incongruity. When someone cracks up laughing at something, then, and someone else solemnly says, "That's not funny," it is not as if one had said, "That's a cherry tree," and the other, "No it isn't." They are simply registering their different reactions to what has happened. As we'll be saying often in this book, humor lies in how we look at situations.

Humor can occur wherever we have expectations. But it seems to work best where the expectations are about things that are important to us. That's why most comedy plays off expectations about things like cleanliness, hostility, and sex.

The incongruity also works best when what we experience is not just different from what we expect, but opposed to it. In England a minister once wrote this note to his bishop: "I regret to inform you of my wife's death.

29

Can you possibly send me a substitute for the weekend?"
The humor here is based on the clash between the two
possible meanings for "substitute"—fill-in religious
leader, and fill-in sex partner. If the note had read: "I
regret to inform you of my son's death. Can you possibly
send me a substitute for the weekend?" it would not have
been funny.

In the business world, clashes of meanings like this
can be expensive. In the 1960s, for example, General
Motors decided to market its popular Chevrolet Nova in
Latin America, but sales were dismal. Finally, someone
figured out why: in Spanish, Nova sounds like the words
"No va," meaning "It doesn't go." Ford had similar problems with sales of the Caliente, which is Spanish slang
for "prostitute," and the Pinto, slang for "small penis."

When Electrolux vacuum cleaners were first marketed
in Sweden, the Swedes created this slogan for the box:
"Nothing Sucks Like Electrolux."

Humor Is Not the Same as Joy or Optimism

Once we understand that humor is enjoying incongruity, we can understand some things that most books on
humor misunderstand. It is that humor is not necessarily
joyful or even optimistic.

People who laugh a lot are often thought to have an
unrealistic, pie-in-the-sky attitude that everything is
going great. Many managers I've known who prided
themselves on their hard-headed realism, are suspicious
of humor because they associate it with mindless optimism. Remember the foolish confidence of the first two
little pigs in their song "Who's Afraid of the Big Bad
Wolf?" And many books on humor perpetuate this mis-

taken association. If you're looking around a bookstore, you can spot them right away. Just look for the balloons and/or "Have a Nice Day" happy faces on the cover.

After eighteen years of research into humor, I am convinced that there's nothing essentially optimistic about it. Personally, I am critical of most of our society's institutions, and am pessimistic about most of our problems. I still laugh a lot. In fact, my sharp eye for stupidity, irrationality, hypocrisy, tackiness, folly, and other human shortcomings is a big part of my sense of humor. Pollyanna types who see the world through rose-colored glasses may be content and pleasant, but they usually have little or no sense of humor.

In general, humor thrives not on the positive but on the negative aspects of situations. As Mark Twain said, laughter springs from suffering—there will be no humor in heaven.

When we find a situation funny, there is a certain delight we feel, but that enjoyment need not be—in fact usually isn't—happiness with the way things are, or with the way they will be. What we are enjoying is some incongruity, some clash between what we expected and what we experienced. And, let's face it, most of the time when the world does not match our expectations, it's not by being better than we expected but by being worse. Murphy's Law, "If anything can go wrong, it will," is an exaggeration, but contains a fundamental insight into the human condition. That's why it has spawned hundreds of corollaries, such as:

- It is impossible for an optimist to be pleasantly surprised.

31

- In order for something to become clean, something else must become dirty.

- If you don't care where you are, you aren't lost.

- The other line moves faster.[3]

Humor can be as hard-headed, realistic, and even pessimistic as you like. The person with the sharp sense of humor tends to see more, not fewer, problems than most people see, and tends to play up their severity. Think of Mark Twain, Dorothy Parker, Woody Allen, or Rita Rudner. They are not Pollyannas, but highly critical observers of real life with all its warts. Or consider this simple epitaph from a colonial graveyard in Massachusetts:

I TOLD YOU I WAS SICK.

Humorists don't hide from incompetence, mistakes, or even disasters. Indeed, some of the best humor points out how bad situations really are. On my next trip to the bookstore, I'm going to hunt down the book with this intriguing title: *The Situation Is Hopeless But Not Serious: A Guide to Unhappiness*.

Now the spirit of humor does have a certain good cheer to it, but that's not joy or even optimism. Indeed, the main value of humor is precisely that it lets us face our problems realistically. With a sense of humor we ride out the storm, not by deceiving ourselves that everything is going great, but by keeping our cool and our sense of perspective. The same mental jolt that blows away other people, we enjoy.

The hard-headed realism of humor and its power to help us cope with difficult situations come across in a story told by Dr. Douglas Lindsey, in his presentation on "Humor in the Emergency Room" at a humor conference several years ago.

> The young man was brought in with a bullet hole over his heart, was admitted in coma, and promptly died. I picked up a scalpel, opened his chest from here to here, put my finger over the hole, and squeezed his heart a few times. It started. So off we go to the operating room, with me walking along one hand in the chest. On the way he woke up, raised his head to see what was going on, comprehended what he saw, and made a remark of high pertinence: "My blood type is A-positive." Whereupon the efficient nurse broke in with: "Hey, Jack, before you go back to sleep would you sign the operative permit?" Which he did. In medical circles this is known as "informed consent."

In telling this story, Dr. Lindsey didn't exaggerate or use any comedian's tricks, but this life-and-death situation came across as full of humor. Lindsey's appreciation of that humor was certainly not mindless optimism; it was as realistic as could be. In the emergency room he was not denying the man's serious condition, nor "laughing off" his responsibility to give him the best medical treatment he could. On the contrary, he was using all his skills superbly. He was taking the situation seriously, without taking it solemnly. His sense of humor let him see what was going on from a higher, more rational perspective, so that he could keep his cool and do just what had to be done. His sense of humor made him a better physician.

Funny Ha-Ha, Funny Strange, and Negative Emotions

So far we have been looking at humor as the enjoyment of incongruity. But we do not always enjoy incongruity, of course. Often when something surprises us, we are anything but amused. If I answered a knock at the door to find a shotgun pointed at my face, for example, that would be incongruous but hardly funny. Instead of enjoying the incongruity, I'd be bothered by it.

There are two main ways of being bothered by something incongruous—I call them puzzlement and negative emotions. Let's consider them one at a time to see how they differ from humor.

In being puzzled, something doesn't fit our mental patterns, and we feel challenged to make it fit. What wasn't supposed to happen happens, and we try to figure out why. We may proceed by inspecting things, reviewing our information, or asking experts. If we solve the puzzle, we feel relieved, and this feeling can be pleasant—ask any research scientist, or someone who does crossword or jigsaw puzzles.

Puzzlement and amusement are often close. The word "funny," in fact, has two meanings: funny strange and funny ha-ha. Anything new, different, or strange can be puzzling under the right conditions. Even something intended to be funny might instead be puzzling to some people. Babies, for instance, often do not laugh when adults play tricks on them, because instead of enjoying the surprise, they are trying to figure out what happened. Or consider the Charles Addams cartoon on the following page, first published in *The New Yorker* in 1940.

Drawing by Chas. Addams; © 1940, 1968

The New Yorker Magazine, Inc.

It was a hit, and so after World War II it was published in Europe. But when it appeared in a German magazine, over a dozen readers wrote in with their solutions. Instead of laughing, they put on their thinking caps and came up with ideas like this: "As she approached the tree, she released one of her skiis, and then she got back into it on the other side of the tree." These readers saw the same incongruous drawing you just saw, but they saw it as a puzzle, not as a cartoon. Similarly, when somebody's computer at work unexpectedly starts printing out hundreds of Zs, you might be laughing while someone else stands there solemnly puzzled, trying to figure out what happened.

So being puzzled is one alternative to being amused when we experience the incongruous. The other alternative I call negative emotions, my general term for fear, anger, sadness, and the like.

Many cases of incongruity which bring on negative emotions involve a threat. Here we have a practical concern about the incongruity. Things are slipping out of our control, and we want to bring them back into control, back to the way they "should be." In emotions like anger and fear, there are changes in our bodies to prepare us to regain control, either by fighting or by running away— we become more alert, our hearts beat faster, and our muscles are energized.

Although we do not experience such bodily changes in puzzlement, in many ways puzzlement is like negative emotions. In both we feel a loss of control that makes us uneasy. So we want to change something. In negative emotions we want the incongruous situation to be differ- ent—we want the danger to be gone, the failure to be a success, or whatever. In puzzlement we want to change not the incongruous situation but our understanding of it: we want to know more so that the situation fits into our picture of the world. If today's mail brought a letter threatening my life, for example, I would react to this incongruous situation with fear. What I would want to change is my being in danger. But if instead I received an anonymous cashier's check for a million dollars, I would react with puzzlement. What I would want to change is not my receiving the check, but my ignorance about who sent it.

Both puzzlement and negative emotions, however, are quite different from amusement. When we are amused we are not bothered by what has happened. We do not feel a disturbing loss of control as in puzzlement and in negative emotions. Even physically, laughter is quite different from negative emotions and puzzlement. Negative emotions and puzzlement make us more tense and motivate us to act, either to eliminate the problem or to solve the puzzle. We even have hormones like epinephrine (adrenaline) to get us going. Laughter, on the other hand, gets us to relax rather than tense up, and does not motivate us to do anything. While anger is preparation for fighting, and fear is preparation for running away or defending ourselves, laughter isn't preparation for doing anything. Indeed, it's physically incapacitating. We lose muscle tension and control—in heavy laughter we may wet our pants and fall on the floor.

Humor and Mental Distance

But if humor, puzzlement, and negative emotions are all reactions to incongruous situations, what determines which reaction we will have in any particular situation? When something out of the ordinary happens, how come one person is laughing, another person is puzzled, and someone else is getting scared or angry?

The main factor at work here I call "mental distance." When we are right in the middle of a situation so that it fills our attention, we tend to be very concerned that everything goes as we expect, and that we understand everything that's going on. In that frame of mind even small incongruities can seem threatening, and so what-ever surprises us is likely to puzzle us, scare us, make us angry, or upset us in some other way. But if we can look at things from farther back, in the bigger picture, so that they do not fill our attention and we are not overwhelmed with concern, we will see them more objectively and be more likely to laugh.

Did you ever watch a colony of ants hard at work? If those little insects could think, they would undoubtedly take themselves seriously. Each time one dropped the piece of leaf it was carrying, it would get upset. But as we watch all their little comings and goings from our higher, disengaged perspective, the whole colony can look funny. Similarly, in our own lives, as we step back from disturbing situations, seeing them more objectively and less subjectively, they often seem funny. Remember losing that crummy job you had in high school? Viewing things close up and short term, you may have thought of that event as awful, but from a little distance you were probably able to see its comic side.

Last December our seven-year-old son Jordan came down with pneumonia. We took him to the doctor and got him started on antibiotics. Jordan's teacher very thoughtfully set aside an art class for his classmates to make him get-well cards, and one of the kids dropped off the cards at our house. The first four or five cards brought smiles to Jordan's face, but then he got to Allison McAndrew's card (see page 39).

Reading the card, Jordan started weeping. My wife and I read the last line as "Your friend Allison McAndrew," but he read it as "You're fried, Allison McAndrew." Even the artwork upset him. "That flower's dead, isn't it, Dad?" he asked. "And that horse—is it in a cemetery?" Then he reread the top of the card, and putting his head in his hands, lamented, "If she didn't want me to know, why did she tell me?"

Allison McAndrew's Card for Jordan

I was biting my cheeks to keep from laughing in Jordan's face; my wife had to leave the room. From our higher perspective we knew that Jordan's pneumonia was going to pass and so Allison's message was alarmist. With this mental distance, we could laugh. But Jordan had no distance from his situation, and so for him it was deeply tragic.

There are several ways in which we get distance from situations. I group the main ones into four categories:

•Distance of Fiction

•Distance in Space

•Distance in Time

•Personal Distance

The first of these is the distance between fiction and reality. Many situations that are not funny in real life become funny in jokes, cartoons, and comedies. The violent stunts of Road Runner and Wile E. Coyote, or the Three Stooges, would be painful and distressing in real life, but in their fictional setting they are comic. The most popular single-frame cartoon in history, Gary Larsen's *Far Side*, was full of people and animals hurting and killing each other. In one *Far Side* captioned simply "Tethercat," two dogs have tied a cat to a long rope hung from a pole, and they are batting it back and forth. If we saw two children torturing a cat in that way, of course, we would be disgusted and try to stop them. And yet almost everyone but the most serious cat-lover can chuckle when this event is fictionalized in a cartoon. Similarly, comedians often exaggerate the disappointment and suffering in the stories they tell. That makes it clear that what they are saying is at least partly fictional, allowing the audience to get some distance from the events being described. That way we can enjoy the story, rather than be disturbed by it.

The second kind of distance that makes room for humor is spatial distance. We often laugh about far away events reported in the newspaper, even though they might not be funny if they were closer to home. Just leaving a troubling situation sometimes gives us the spatial distance we need to laugh. Did you ever visit a city, have a stressful time there, and then get in an airplane to fly home? As the plane rose higher and higher, and the people, the cars, and then the buildings became tiny specks, did you laugh or at least smile, as you felt the distance increase?

The third kind of distance is distance in time, the disengagement we have from events in the past. Think of the funny stories you tell when you get together with old friends. Aren't many of them about events that didn't seem funny at all when they were happening? In fact I'll bet that the funniest stories you tell are about precisely the things that were most disturbing at the time. As Steve Allen put it,

Tragedy + time = comedy.

An event at a particular moment that frustrated or scared you, or made you mad, is funny now that you can look back on it as safely in the past.

Here's an example of distance in time, a newspaper story from 1989:

> Courthouse toilets explode after lines get
> crossed   –© The Associated Press
>
> SEATTLE—About two dozen toilets and uri-
> nals in the King County Courthouse exploded
> when they were flushed Thursday because an
> air compressor had been erroneously con-
> nected to a water line, officials said.
>
> "We think we lost about 20 to 25 toilets,"
> said building manager Bill Kemp. No injuries
> were reported, although several people appar-
> ently were soaked.

Reprinted courtesy of The Associated Press

Now as these toilets were blowing up, I doubt that any of the people on them were amused. If you can't count on the toilets, after all, what can you count on? But I'll bet that shortly after the explosion lots of those people were laughing, and within an hour, all but the grumpiest found it funny. An even safer bet is that today, years later, if you asked those involved in the Seattle Courthouse Toilet Explosion to list the three funniest events in their lives, virtually all of them would include this one.

The fourth kind of distance that makes humor possible is personal distance, the difference between one person and another. Many situations that are funny when we see them happening to someone else are not funny when they happen to us. Mel Brooks was exaggerating but not completely off the mark when he said, "Tragedy is me cutting my finger; comedy is you falling down a manhole and dying." To see how personal distance works, consider another newspaper story.

Battered burglar picked on the wrong nuns, police say   –© Gannett News Service

WILMINGTON, Del.—A burglar here picked on the wrong nuns, police said, and he has the cuts and bruises to prove it.

Sister Kathleen Halpin stumbled upon a burglar in St. Paul's Convent about 3 a.m. yesterday, and he started hitting her. She hit him back. Before long, six more Franciscan nuns joined the fray.

His face cut and teeth broken, the burglar fled the convent, into the arms of Wilmington police.

Angel Vasquez, 24, was charged with burglary, criminal mischief, assault, and two counts of offensive touching.

Reprinted courtesy of the Gannett Rochester Newspapers

Now this story is written to be funny, but I'm sure that when Angel Vasquez talks about the event, it's not as comedy, but as tragedy or at least melodrama. He probably describes what happened as a beating, which it was. The newspaper reporter, though, kept us from identifying and sympathizing with Angel Vasquez, so that we would be able to find the story funny. This personal distance was created largely by describing him as the bad guy who didn't deserve our sympathy—a burglar picking on nuns.

Once we understand the emotional disengagement in humor, we can see how humor can be a bad thing or a good thing. It's a bad thing when we are disengaged from problems we should be doing something about. In an emergency where someone needs our help, sympathetic emotions are what's called for, and then it's wrong to stand back and laugh.

Humor can be a good thing, on the other hand, when a disengaged, more objective perspective is called for. This can be true even in situations like the one presented earlier of the doctor in the emergency room treating the man with the bullet hole over his heart. The doctor's sense of humor allowed him to not be overcome by panic, which would interfere with doing what had to be done. His sense of humor kept his emotions under control and his head clear, and so helped him save the man's life.

There are situations, too, where someone faces a major problem, but nothing can be done about it. Here humor may be not only permissible but a psychologically healthy way of coping. A nurse in one of my seminars told me of a patient with cancer of the penis whom she was preparing for surgery. Knowing that this man was about to have his penis removed, she was nervous and couldn't think what to say. Finally, just as the surgeon was about to come into the room, she blurted out, "It won't be long now." "You got that right!" the patient said with a laugh.

Or consider the seventy-six-year-old man whose spreading cancer had required so much surgery that his weight had gone from 200 to under 100. Through it all he never lost his sense of humor. "They could make another old fart out of the pieces they've taken out of me," he quipped.[4]

Now we may not have to face cancer surgery, but we all face a much more severe loss—our death. And just because death is the unavoidable end of everyone's life, there are countless jokes about it. Well past the age of ninety-five, George Burns entertained audiences, often using this opening line: "It's nice to be here. At my age, it's nice to be anywhere!" Even people who were about to die have seen humor in their situation. Some of my favorite last words came from Sir Thomas More, who was beheaded for disagreeing with King Henry VIII. With his rheumatism, More was having trouble climbing the stairs of the executioner's block, so he asked the executioner, "Could you give me a hand getting up? I'll be able to get down by myself." That quip showed not only courage but an admirable objectivity about his own life and death. Instead of being overcome with useless self-pity, he looked at the situation from a distance, and saw it as funny.

All the kinds of distance we have been discussing— the distance of fiction, distance in space, distance in time, and personal distance—are unique to humans. And that's why we are the only animals that laugh. The lower animals have no distance from their world, but are locked into their immediate experience, into here and now and into what is real and practical. They are also locked into their own individual perspectives, unable to see themselves objectively, from the outside. When they are surprised, they react only with puzzlement or negative emotions. Alone among the animals, we are able to unhook our thinking from the here and now and real and practical, and from our personal perspectives. This ability to rise above our immediate experience gave us not only humor but also our abstract thinking in mathematics and the sciences, and our many forms of fiction and play—sports, drama, dance, art, literature, and the rest. As we go through this book, we'll see how our uniquely human ability to distance ourselves from our experience—especially as we face problems— allows us to cope and even prosper in what would otherwise be a pretty threatening world.

LAUGHTER OR TEARS: A GROUP EXERCISE

Exercise 2-1

1. Think of something that happened at work that you tell as a funny story. Now pretend for a moment that you just lost your sense of humor completely. Describe the same event so that instead of sounding funny, it sounds upsetting. (With some events you can do this by taking a purely practical attitude, and emphasizing the time or money wasted. With other events, you can pretend that you are ultra-sensitive, and emphasize how your feelings were hurt.) Give everyone a chance to tell his or her formerly funny story as an upsetting story.

2. Now do things the other way around. Think of something at work that has upset you recently—say, some habit of your boss's, or some mistake that someone else made that you had to correct. Pretend that you're Roseanne or Bill Cosby or your favorite comedian, and talk about this problem, so that it sounds at least partly funny. Give everyone a chance to tell his or her formerly upsetting story as a funny story.

3. Discuss what made the difference between the funny viewpoint and the upsetting viewpoint in these stories. What can we learn here that will be useful the next time something potentially upsetting happens?

What can we learn here that will be useful the next time something potentially upsetting happens?

Notes

[1] John Morreall, ed., *The Philosophy of Laughter and Humor* (Albany: State University of New York Press, 1987). John Morreall, *Taking Laughter Seriously* (Albany: State University of New York Press, 1983).

[2] In Morreall, ed., *The Philosophy of Laughter and Humor*, p. 19.

[3] Arthur Block, ed., *Murphy's Law, Book Two* (Los Angeles: Price/Stern/Sloan, 1984), pp. 14-20.

[4] C.W. Metcalf and Roma Felible, *Lighten Up: Survival Skills for People under Pressure* (Reading, MA: Addison-Wesley, 1992), p. 30.

CHAPTER 3

LAUGH FOR THE HEALTH OF IT

W hen people who live past age 100 are asked the secret of their longevity, they often mention their frequent laughter. Dr. Kenneth Pelletier, author of *Longevity: Fulfilling Our Biological Potential,*[1] studied cultures where many people claim to be 120 to 150 years old, in Pakistan, central Asia, the Sudan, Ecuador, and Mexico. He found that these cultures shared certain worldviews, values, and emotional traits, including high esteem for old people and a belief in a purposeful universe. Most striking of all, Pelletier says, is their customary humor, vitality, and joyfulness.

Many cultures have folk sayings to the effect that laughter is healthy. Even the Bible, whose references to laughter are mostly negative, has Proverbs 17:22: "A merry heart doeth good like a medicine, but a brittle spirit drieth the bones."

In the 13th century, the French surgeon Henri de Mondeville joked with his patients after surgery because he believed that laughter would aid their recovery. In the 18th century, Lord Shaftesbury, suggested that laughter is good for the nervous system because it releases nervous energy. The philosopher Immanuel Kant said that laughter is beneficial because it massages the internal organs. And in his 1928 book *Laughter and Health*, the American physician James Walsh observed that laughter following surgery seems to promote healing and reduce pain.

Until recently, however, ideas like these were just folklore. Almost no one took laughter seriously enough to do any research. Fortunately, the medical community had Dr. William Fry, Jr. of Stanford University Medical School, who began studying the physical benefits of laughter in the 1960s. Thanks to his pioneering work, a number of researchers are now investigating the many connections between humor and health.

In this chapter, we'll discuss some individual medical benefits of laughter and humor, and in the next chapter we'll see how humor works against the group of physical and psychological symptoms called stress.

One benefit of laughter is the way muscles contract in the abdomen, chest, shoulders, and face. The effect on these muscles is like moderate exercise.

Laughter also gives the lungs a workout. When we laugh heartily we take in six times more oxygen than when we are talking. In fact, simply smiling makes it easier to breathe. Try this exercise.

BREATHING WITH THREE FACES

Exercise 3-1

Pretend that you're an actor, and you have to make some faces.

1. The first is a bland face. You are not experiencing any emotions at all, and your face is relaxed and passive. With this bland face, take a deep breath and then exhale. Repeat inhaling and exhaling twice. Note the effort it takes to breathe with a bland face.

2. Your second face is an angry face. Pretend that someone just cut you off in traffic, almost crashing into you. Make your face express total anger. With this angry face, take a deep breath and then exhale. Repeat inhaling and exhaling twice. Note the effort it takes to breathe with an angry face.

3. Your third face is a smiling face. Pretend that a young child just gave you a funny gift. Let a big smile come over you. With this smiling face, take a deep breath and then exhale. Repeat inhaling and exhaling twice. Note the effort it takes to breathe with a smiling face.

Undoubtedly, you noticed that a smiling face feels better than an angry face or a bland face, but did you also notice how much easier it is to breathe with a smiling face?

In laughter, too, the heart pumps more, increasing blood circulation. Twenty seconds of hearty laughter, Dr. Fry estimates, gives the heart the same exercise as three minutes of hard rowing.

Another benefit of laughter is the relaxation it brings. That wonderful "Whew!" we experience after laughing hard isn't just a feeling. While we are laughing, muscle tension, heart rate, and blood pressure rise, but when we stop, they all drop to levels lower than before we started laughing. And this relaxation lasts up to forty-five minutes.

The brain is also affected by laughter, largely through the hormones that laughter triggers. Catecholamine, which heightens alertness and may reduce inflammation, is released, and it triggers endorphins, the body's own pain killers.

Pain can also be reduced by the muscle relaxation that laughter brings. Muscle tension increases pain; in fact the two can get into a vicious cycle, as in some headaches. The pain causes stress and the muscles tighten. That brings on muscle spasms, which cause more pain, which causes more tension, then more pain, and so on. Laughter can interrupt this cycle, and so reduce pain.[2]

Humor, especially active joking, has also been shown to increase tolerance for pain. In one experiment, people holding their hands in ice water were able to stand the discomfort longer if they joked about it.[3] In another experiment with passive humor, those who laughed while listening to a comedy tape were then able to tolerate higher levels of pressure in a blood pressure cuff before reporting discomfort.[4]

Much of the recent medical research into the pain-relieving properties of laughter, and into the benefits of humor generally, was prompted by Norman Cousins' book *Anatomy of an Illness as Perceived by the Patient*.[5]

Working under a lot of stress as editor of *The Saturday Review*, Cousins developed an acute form of arthritis, *ankylosing spondylitis*, in which the tissue between the vertebrae breaks down and the vertebrae gradually fuse. Cousins was in almost constant pain, and at the worst point of his illness, his jaws were almost locked. The doctors gave him a 1-in-500 chance of recovery. Unwilling to accept those odds, Cousins took charge of his own treatment. He figured that it was the stress and negative emotions in his life that had gotten him into this disease, and so it would be relaxation, laughter, and positive emotions that would get him out. Cousins left the hospital—"no place for a sick person," he quipped—and checked into a hotel across the street, where he had a full-time nurse. In addition to large amounts of vitamin C, he prescribed for himself daily doses of laughter. His friend Allen Funt, producer of the *Candid Camera* TV show, brought over tapes from the show, along with Marx Brothers movies and other funny stuff. Cousins' laughter relieved his pain. Ten minutes of belly laughter brought him two hours of pain-free sleep. His laughter, along with the vitamin C, good medical care, relaxation, and the support of family and friends, eventually brought about a full recovery.

Recent research has uncovered what is perhaps the most important influence of laughter on health—its enhancement of the immune system, our body's built-in defenses against infections. All around us are bacteria, viruses, and other germs that can cause disease. Staying healthy is not living in a germ-free world, but living with germs in such a way that we keep them from multiplying inside us. We also have to kill off the malignant cells produced by our own bodies. To handle these jobs, our bone marrow, lymph glands, spleen, thymus, and liver produce substances to police our bodies, eliminating harmful germs and cells. "Natural killer cells" patrol our bodies, destroying viruses and some kinds of cancer cells. To protect our nasal passages and throats from infection, we have germ-fighters called immunoglobulins in the mucus lining of these passages. Our white blood cells also kill off dangerous bacteria—we sometimes notice them in action by the swollen lymph glands on either side of our throats.

Anything that affects our immune system can affect our health. In the condition known as AIDS, the immune system is greatly or totally suppressed. A milder suppression can occur when we are under a lot of stress. The death of a spouse, for example, can greatly reduce the ability of the immune system to fight off disease. That's why widows and widowers sometimes die months after their spouses. The traditional way of describing this was that the person "died of a broken heart." The more technical description is that the loss of the spouse suppressed the survivor's immune system, and the individual was unable to withstand illness.

Fortunately, the immune system can be enhanced as well as suppressed, and humor enhances it. Studies by Dr. Lee Berk of Loma Linda University have shown that mirthful laughter is associated with increased activity in several parts of the immune system: the number of B lymphocytes; the number of activated T lymphocytes; the number of antibodies carrying immunoglobulin A, G, and M; the number and activity of natural killer cells; and the amount of gamma interferon. People who laugh a lot have a higher level of immunoglobulin-A in their throats and nasal passages and so come down with fewer colds than people who seldom laugh. One study found that new mothers who laughed a lot had fewer upper respiratory infections, and that their babies did too!

Not only does humor help our immune system fight off disease, but when we are already ill, it can improve our attitude during recovery. As Norman Cousins pointed out, finding out that you have a serious illness can cause you to panic, and that reaction itself can constrict blood vessels and cause harmful biochemical changes. By getting us to loosen up, humor can block a panic reaction and the damage it would do.

In years to come, medical science will undoubtedly find that laughter and humor have still other benefits. For example, a few researchers are now looking into the laxative effect of laughter. One of them, Dr. Patt Schwab, playfully suggests that this may be why (subconsciously?) people keep joke books on the back of their toilets. But from the pioneering research that has already been done, we know that laughter, if not the best medicine, as *Reader's Digest* calls it, is at least healthy for you.

And while research on the healthiness of humor has just begun, hospitals have been putting humor to use for over a decade. As Vera Robinson, author of *Humor and the Health Professions,*[6] has noted, almost everything in the hospital tends to create anxiety in patients. They are asked by total strangers to take off their clothes, they are poked and prodded and jabbed with needles and tubes, they are awakened to be given sleeping pills. The whole experience is disorienting, disconcerting, and even humiliating. A little humor from the medical staff can go a long way to make patients relax and feel more at home. It can express support for them and what they are feeling, open up channels of communication, and serve as a safety valve for their anxiety, frustration, or anger.

One of the interactions hospital patients miss most is humor in conversation. In one study, four out of five terminally ill patients said that they wished people would stop being so glum and joke with them.

Debbie Lieber, head of a group of nurses called the NFL, Nurses for Laughter, was one of the first to intentionally put humor into health care. She and her colleagues designated one day Professional Cap Day. Instead of wearing nurses' caps, they wore their regular uniforms with baseball caps, construction helmets, and other professional headgear. This simple idea cost nothing, but brought a spirit of fun into the hospital which the patients and staff appreciated.

For a long time children's wards have used clowns, but now many hospitals provide humor for adults too. Some have movie comedies on closed circuit TV. Many have comedy carts with funny books, magazines, audio and video tapes, and games. At Albuquerque Hospital the maintenance man built a comedy cart to look like a vendor's pushcart, and painted it with bright floral designs. Leslie Gibson started with one comedy cart at

Morton Plant Hospital in Clearwater, Florida, but is now up to a dozen. Some hospitals have also put in humor rooms and play rooms, which they find well used by patients' families, who often feel more scared and emotionally drained than the patients themselves.

The response of patients to humor has been overwhelmingly positive. They adjust better to their stay in the hospital, they report better rapport and communication with the medical staff, and their recovery time is shorter. Some hospitals have been so impressed with these results that they have hired humor consultants to coordinate their humor activities.

The enthusiasm of nurses for humor is indicated by the subscriber list for *The Journal of Nursing Jocularity*, currently at over 30,000. Canada has a humor magazine for nurses called *Stitches*. There have been many regional and national conferences on humor for nurses.

No one has done more to encourage the use of humor in medicine than Norman Cousins, who was mentioned earlier. After humor helped in his own recovery, Cousins quit his stressful job to become an adjunct professor at the medical school of the University of California at Los Angeles. There he worked as educator and counselor with staff, patients, and families of patients. More than 4,200 physicians have written to him of their own experiences with the power of positive emotions. Cousins' inspiring message and many wonderful stories can be found in his books *Anatomy of an Illness as Perceived by the Patient* and *Head First: The Biology of Hope*.[7] His own humanity shines through his clear writing, and his sense of humor is never far below the surface. In fact, I can think of no better way to close this chapter on the healthiness of humor than with a story about a joke Cousins played during one of his stays in the hospital.

After breakfast the nurse came in with a urine specimen bottle for him to fill. When she left for a moment, he took the apple juice from his breakfast tray and poured it into the bottle. She came back and he handed her the bottle. With a troubled look on her face she said, "Gee, Mr. Cousins, it looks awfully cloudy this morning." "You're right," he said, taking the bottle back and raising it to his lips, "let's run it through again." And he drank it.

Notes

[1] Kenneth Pelletier, *Longevity: Fulfilling Our Biological Potential* (New York: Dell, 1982).

[2] Paul E. McGhee, *The Laughter Remedy: Health, Healing and the Amuse System* (self-published, 1991), p. 57.

[3] Ofra Nevo, Giora Keinan, and Mina Teshimovsky-Arditi, "Humor and Pain Tolerance." *Humor: International Journal of Humor Research*, 6 (1993), pp. 71-88.

[4] R. Cogan and others, "Effects of laughter and relaxation on discomfort thresholds," *Journal of Behavioral Medicine*, 10 (1987), pp. 139-144.

[5] Norman Cousins, *Anatomy of an Illness as Perceived by the Patient* (New York: Norton, 1979).

[6] Vera Robinson, *Humor and the Health Professions*, 2nd ed. (Thorofare, NJ: Slack, 1991).

[7] Norman Cousins, *Anatomy of an Illness as Perceived by the Patient* (New York: Norton, 1979), and *Head First: The Biology of Hope* (New York: E.P. Dutton, 1989).

CHAPTER 4

HUMOR IS THE OPPOSITE OF STRESS

I n discussing how humor enhances the immune system, we mentioned that stress suppresses the immune system. But humor and stress work against each other in other ways as well. In fact, to understand the benefits of humor, it's useful to look at the general opposition between humor and stress.

We sometimes talk of humor and stress as mental events, but they are also physical, and their physical aspects are intimately related to their mental aspects. Humor is not just an event in the mind or brain; it involves our diaphragm, lungs, muscles, heart, and immune system, too. Stress happens not only in the mind and brain, but in the nervous system generally, the endocrine system, the circulatory system, the immune system, and the muscles. It involves powerful hormones such as epinephrine (adrenaline) and norepinephrine (noradrenaline), which cause changes like muscle tension, faster heartbeat, and increased blood pressure.

Stress: the Epidemic

In the 1990s stress has reached epidemic proportions in this country. Stress-related claims by white-collar workers in California increased 700 percent during the

1980s. A large proportion of our population is literally worried sick. The American Academy of Family Physicians estimates that two-thirds of visits to the family doctor are prompted by stress-related symptoms. Stress is a major contributor to six of the leading causes of death, including heart disease and cancer. A study published in 1990 by the American Medical Association found that men suffering job stress were three times more likely to have high blood pressure. As Dr. Joel Elkes, director of the behavioral medicine program at the University of Louisville, commented, "Our mode of life itself, the way we live, is emerging as today's principal cause of illness."[1]

The stressful way we live is based largely on the stressful way we work. Compared to twenty-five years ago, we work more hours a day and bring more work home with us. And in most families now, both adults work, requiring them to squeeze in household duties before and after a long day's work. As women have come into the workforce in large numbers over the last twenty years, the rate of heart attacks in women has increased 100 percent and the rate of peptic ulcers in women is now equal to the rate for men.

Stress in the American workplace has increased for many reasons. Perhaps the most basic is the rapid pace of change. As we'll see in this chapter, stress is a reaction to a perceived threat, and people often feel threatened when their familiar routines are suddenly changed, as when they are asked to do new tasks. The lack of job security caused by the restructuring of corporations and massive layoffs adds to the perceived threat, as do the increased workloads and shorter deadlines placed on those left behind in the "downsized" workplace.

At the beginning of the 1990s, one out of four American workers suffered from anxiety disorders or stress-related illnesses. They lost an average of sixteen days of work each year. A Gallup poll of 210 personnel and medical directors of American corporations found that about the same number of workers suffered from depression. A survey commissioned by the Northwestern National Life Insurance Company in 1991 found that 46 percent of American workers thought of their jobs as "highly stressful" (double the rate from 1985), 34 percent had considered quitting their jobs in 1990 because of the stress, 34 percent said they believed that job stress would lead them to burn out soon, and 14 percent had actually quit their jobs the previous year because of excess stress. Worker's compensation claims based on job stress, almost unheard of in 1980, now represent one-fourth of all claims, and are projected to outnumber all others by the end of the decade. The National Institutes of Health predicts that 52 percent of American executives will die of stress-related illnesses.

Stressed-out workers make more mistakes, have more accidents, are less productive, are absent more, and require more company medical benefits, all of which are estimated to cost American employers $200 billion a year. That's why most employee assistance programs offer information and workshops on stress, and over a quarter of Fortune 500 corporations have stress management programs.

Evidence of stress is everywhere. Already by the early 1980s, U.S. workers were consuming over fifteen tons of aspirin and aspirin substitutes a day. Our three best-selling prescription drugs were Tagamet (for ulcers), Inderal (for high blood pressure), and Valium (no explanation needed).[2] Do you or a colleague have a desk drawer for stress remedies such as Tums, Maalox, and Mylanta? Our nation's high rate of alcoholism is also evidence that we feel a need to relax, to "take the edge off reality," as an alcoholic friend of mine puts it.

Stress can manifest itself in many ways, such as headaches, neck pain, muscle spasms, clenched jaws and teeth grinding, ulcers and other stomach disorders, fatigue or complete exhaustion, sleeplessness, and proneness to colds. Emotional and behavioral problems also result from stress, like proneness to accidents, mood swings, the inability to concentrate, reduced contact with friends, and less intimacy with loved ones.

By 1990 there were already 120,000 articles and books on stress, and the number has been increasing steadily since then. Books about stress often command their own shelf in bookstores, with titles that are themselves stressful: *Modern Madness: The Hidden Link between Work and Emotional Conflict, How to Avoid Stress Before It Kills You*, and *Is It Worth Dying for?*

Unless we change the way we work and our attitudes toward work, stress will become an even worse problem, as we can learn from Japan, where overwork and stress are a calculated part of life. The six-day work week is standard in Japan, and few workers take their entire vacations. The average Japanese worker spends twelve hours a day working and commuting. A few years ago, when the government encouraged banks to close on Saturdays, many bank workers began staying three or four hours late during the week. Where has this workaholism gotten these workers? The Japanese traditionally are reluctant to complain about their companies, but in a 1991 survey 90 percent of businessmen and working women reported that they suffer chronic fatigue. Stress and overwork are at such high levels that one-fourth of Japanese workers say they fear *karoshi*—death from overwork—which takes the lives of 10,000 Japanese executives each year. In one eight-month period in 1987 the presidents of ten major Japanese companies died of stress-related illnesses. The Japanese government now has a National Council for Victims of Karoshi. Hiroshi Kawahito, the head of the council's office in Tokyo, states the problem bluntly: "Japanese are sacrificing their health, and all too often their lives, for the sake of their companies."[3]

Stress is not something we leave at work. A recent survey done by the nation's largest medical liability insurance company showed that problems at work are more likely than personal problems to negatively affect *both* work life and home life. And with increased time pressure at home due to both parents working outside the home, family life is increasingly stressful. Even the youngest children are now affected. When my son was in preschool, we asked him at dinner one night what he had learned that day. He said that he had learned about "handling stress." Putting his finger to the side of his nose, he showed us. "You breathe in one side of your nose and breathe out the other side—so you relax." Here was a group of four-year-olds learning yoga for stress management!

Many techniques are now used for handling stress, including breathing exercises, meditation, massage, mental imaging, bio-feedback, and aerobic exercise. We're going to be considering one of the easiest, cheapest, and most enjoyable: humor.

What Is Stress?

The most basic description of stress is that it is a way of reacting to events. It is our body's arousal to deal with a perceived threat. Stress involves one or both of two emotions, fear and anger. To understand them, we need to say something about emotions in general.

In human beings, an emotion has four components. It begins with a perception or thought. When I feel fear as my car skids on an icy bridge, for example, my thought is that I am going to crash. When I am angry at someone, my thought is that this person has wronged me. Our thought triggers the other three components of the emotion. First is the bodily disturbances, such as the pounding heart and increased muscle tension in fear and anger. Second is our sensations of these disturbances. In fear and anger we feel our muscles getting tighter; that's what our "feeling tense" is. In fear, too, as the blood leaves our hands and feet, they feel cold. In anger, as the blood rushes to our head, our head feels hot. That's why "got cold feet" means that someone was afraid, and calling someone "hot-headed" means that they get angry a lot. And the third effect of the thought is our urge to do something. In fear, for example, we have the urge to fight whatever is threatening us, or to run away from it. In anger, we have the urge to attack the person who is making us angry.

Human emotions can get quite sophisticated, but our basic emotions go back in evolution to the days of the early mammals. For the lower animals, emotions are survival techniques to help them avoid danger, reproduce, and generally keep their species going.

The emotions involved in stress—fear and anger—are two of the oldest emotions, and they evolved to help animals handle threatening situations in which they have to escape danger or overcome obstacles. Fear and anger are our bodies' preparation to run away or to fight.

In the lower animals and in ancient humans, fear and anger were useful emotions. Pretend for a moment that it's 20,000 B.C. and you are a cave-dweller. You come home after a hard day hunting and gathering food, to find a saber-toothed tiger emerging from your cave. Here's a physical challenge to which you must respond quickly, and your body reacts with what in the 20th century would be called stress.

Your eyes and ears open wide to see what's going on. Your muscles tense up. If your dominant emotion is fear, your adrenal glands shoot epinephrine (adrenaline) into your bloodstream, causing your heart to beat faster and stronger. Your blood pressure goes up. Breathing is quicker and more shallow. Your metabolism and the level of sugar in your blood go up to give you the extra energy you'll need for running away or fighting. Your blood changes so that it will clot more easily, should you be injured. Blood rich in oxygen is shunted away from your hands and feet, and from your skin, to the large muscles required for running or fighting. All these changes in fear are useful: they prepare you to handle the danger.

Facing the saber-toothed tiger, your dominant emotion might be anger rather than fear, and it too would be useful. Anger involves a set of physical changes that prepare you for action, in this case fighting rather than fleeing. The anger hormone, norepinephrine, makes you aggressive and more powerful, by raising the level of your blood sugar and making your heart pump more oxygen to your muscles and head.

Now as long as survival depends only on hunting and fighting, fear and anger are useful, as they are in the lower animals. In fact, even today, if we face a simple physical challenge, these emotions can help. Some football coaches try to get their players angry, for example, in order to energize them to run faster and tackle harder. Or think of the story that appears in the tabloid newpapers every year or so, of the woman who comes out to the garage to call her son or husband for dinner, only to discover that the car he had been working under has slipped off the jack and is pinning him. She goes into a rage and her extra strength from the hormone norepinephrine enables her to lift the car off his chest.

But what if the challenge we face calls for fine eye-hand coordination instead of brute strength, or careful thinking and negotiation rather than physical action? When our challenge is physical but not simple, or is not physical at all, then the crude responses of anger or fear will probably hurt rather than help. If the coach's team is a chess team, arousing them for fighting will be counterproductive. Or if the mother discovers that her son has cut his hand deeply, rage or terror will be counterproductive. What she needs is a cool head to remember her first aid training, and to get him to a hospital.

Today almost none of the challenges we face are simple and physical, and so the stress emotions of fear and anger, in which our bodies react as if we were physically threatened, usually only get in the way. This is especially true in the workplace, where most of our challenges require clear-headed thinking and dealing sensitively with other people.

Consider one of our most common fears—the fear of public speaking. In several surveys, people ranked this as their greatest fear (with fear of death coming in number four or five.) Early in human evolution this fear made sense: Standing in an open space with many pairs of eyes focused on you usually meant that you were about to become lunch for a group of predators. In that situation, of course, fear was just the right response: when you noticed all those eyes on you, you got scared and bolted. But what happens when this ancient mechanism kicks in as you are about to give a presentation to fifty colleagues? Your mouth gets dry, your hands cold and sweaty. Your eyes are opened too wide, your face looks blank, your voice comes out strained and weak. You may have prepared your ideas thoroughly and they may be brilliant, but here you are—a stiff, pathetic prey-animal that everyone feels sorry for, just when you wanted to evoke their admiration and respect.

Or take anger in the workplace. When was the last time you blew up at someone at work, and afterward said to yourself, "Wow, that worked great—I should have done that long ago"? Probably never. Can you imagine a situation where following through with anger and *hitting* a colleague or client would be helpful? The question itself sounds silly, doesn't it? When people need to resolve a problem, they need a setting for clear-headed discussion.

In fact, if some of them are angry, the first thing to do is calm them down.

My favorite example of the uselessness of anger is anger in driving. On the road, even the most reasonable people become angry. With my Ph.D. in philosophy and many years of teaching logic, I consider myself rational. But behind the wheel of a car, I revert to Neanderthal man as soon as someone cuts me off or changes lanes without signalling.

There are good explanations for why reasonable people turn Neanderthal behind the wheel. In few of our daily activities are our lives put in such danger by other people, and with little advance warning. For most of us, too, our car is an extension of ourselves. Pulling in front of my car in traffic is cutting *me* off. But even so, anger rarely does any good and usually creates more danger, as well as anger in other drivers.

An enlightening experience a few years ago made it clear to me how futile and dangerous anger can be on the road, as well as how humor can save us from anger. I was driving my pickup truck on the New York State Thruway with my three-year-old son. Chatting along at 65 mph, I glanced in the mirror to see a large trailer truck loaded with steel I-beams less than two feet from the rear end of my truck. The changes that came over me were instantaneous. My heart started pounding, my face got red, and my muscles tightened up. The rational left side of my brain, the language-processing side, nearly shut down, while the right side, the part responsible for auto-matic emotional speech, took over control of my mouth. Strings of prepackaged curses started pouring out. I rolled down my window and extended my left arm above the cab, waving my longest finger furiously. The truck driver, himself no model of rationality, responded in like fashion, laying on his horn, shaking his fist, and generally copying my gorilla behavior. At that, I began steering with my right knee so that I could stick *both* arms out the window and wave both middle fingers. He honked again and pulled out alongside me. Through his open window he challenged me to fight him. Then he pulled ahead of me, put on his air brakes, veered onto the shoulder, and jumped down onto his running board.

One of the awful things about anger, and stress generally, is that your world shrinks. You think of nothing but the problem in front of you, and you have no perspective on it. In my rage, this truck driver filled my attention and thought. Locked into my here and now, I could think of nothing but revenge. I started to pull off the road in front of his truck. But as I came to a stop, a strange liberating thought came to me—I imagined the headline in the next morning's newspaper: "Local Professor Bludgeoned to Death on Thruway." Somehow, miraculously, my imagination had given me a bit of distance from what was happening. Immediately the stranglehold of my anger was broken. I saw my situation more objectively, from a higher perspective—which wasn't that hard. Even my three-year-old had a higher perspective than the truck driver and I had had! The idiocy of what I had done, and was about to do, was now obvious. So I steered my truck back into the driving lane, and accelerated.

Of course, now I had a new problem, because the truck driver had not had a similar mind-opening experience. He was still jumping up and down on his running board. Fortunately, just a quarter-mile ahead was an exit.

I raced to it, paid my toll in record time, and scooted behind the Sunoco station, where my son and I nervously laid low for the next half hour.

Whenever I think of this event, I recall the Irish saying: "You're only a coward for a moment, but you're dead for the rest of your life."

There are two lessons in this story. One is that anger is almost always counterproductive, and the other is that humor blocks anger. I can't be angry with you and simultaneously laughing with you or even laughing about you.

Now in discussing how fear and anger are counterproductive, I have chosen mostly examples in which we "go with" our urge to hit someone, say, or at least come close. But in most stressful situations, of course, we hold back from doing what our bodies are energized to do. Realizing that we shouldn't get violent or run away, we suppress our emotion. So there we are, aroused for action, simmering in our hormones, but with no outlet for our muscle tension and our rising heartbeat and blood pressure.

In one way, of course, it's good that we don't hit anyone or run away. But it's not good for our brains and bodies. Our tension can make us grind our teeth and damage the joints in our jaw. It can cause excess stomach acid and ulcers. It suppresses the activity of our immune system, so that we are more vulnerable to infection and cancer. And over time, our increased blood pressure from stress causes our heart wall to thicken and sets us up for heart attacks. While we may not do as much damage in the workplace as if we had let the emotion take its course, we may do more damage to ourselves.

Whether we let our stressful emotions out *or* hold them in, then, stress is usually harmful.

Humor Works against Stress

With this understanding of stress and the harm it does, we can now see how humor is an antidote to it. Both physically and mentally, laughing about something is the opposite of getting stressed out by it. Before we get into the details, let's start with a simple exercise; see the following page.

Just from the appearance of our bodies, we can see the contrast between stress and humor: stress is tight and oppressive, laughter is loose and liberating. Inside our bodies, too, stress and humor are opposites. When we laugh, levels of chemicals associated with stress, like epinephrine, plasma cortisol, and DOPAC decrease. In the immune system, the levels of natural killer cells and germ-fighting substances like immunoglobulin go down in stress, but go up in laughter. And while immunoglobulin levels decrease in people with a poor sense of humor as they face more problems, people with a good sense of humor suffer no such drop. Humor serves as a buffer against stressful situations which would otherwise suppress the immune system.

Mentally, too, laughter is the opposite of stress. Both are reactions to incongruity, to things not going the way we think they should be going. But in stress we perceive the incongruity as threatening; in humor we do not. And that difference in perception leads to at least three other differences. First, we do not feel the loss of control we

LAUGHTER VS. STRESS

Exercise 4-1

Find a rigid chair, sit up straight in it, and reach down with both hands to grip the edges of the chair tightly. Make every muscle in your body as tense as you can, especially the muscles in your chest, arms, neck, and face. Now, holding that total body tension, laugh loudly.

Could you do it? Not if your brain and body are hooked up in the standard way. You either held the tension and couldn't laugh, or you let go of the tension in order to laugh.

feel in stress. Second, our mental horizons do not shrink to the here and now, as they do in stress. Instead of having tunnel vision in which our current situation fills our attention, we see it from a distance. And third, because we are not obsessed by our situation, we are able to think more clearly.

The loss of control in stress is one of its worst features. Everything seems to be happening *to* us; we're only reacting, not acting. Faced with hassles and problems, stress-prone people tend to turn into passive victims, feeling helpless and acting helpless. And in the victim mode they tend not to think clearly and not to consider all the possibilities open to them. Instead they revert to simple habitual responses. Stress-resistant people, on the other hand, tend to not go into the victim mode, and to feel in greater control of their lives.

Losing our overall feeling of control is damaging to our effectiveness on the job, to our psychological health, and to our physical health. One laboratory experiment with a pair of monkeys is revealing.[4] The two are strapped side by side in chairs. Every so often a light comes on and it is followed by a shock to both monkeys unless the first one turns off the light. The second monkey cannot reach the button for the light, but simply gets shocked if the other monkey doesn't turn off the light, and avoids the shock if the other one does turn it off. In this situation the second monkey goes into the victim mode, passively enduring whatever comes along. While both experience the same shocks, the monkey with no control suffers far more, showing greater physical symptoms of distress than the monkey who has control over the shock.

Human beings experience similar physical and psychological damage from helplessless and stress. In one study, a group of nursing-home residents were for the first time given control of three things: when their lights would be turned on and off, when they had their meals, and when they made and received telephone calls. Over an eighteen-month period, these bits of control resulted in a reduced mortality rate of over 50 percent![5]

In the workplace, having control is similarly important. Studies have shown that secretaries with little control over their jobs are more likely to suffer stress-related illnesses than their bosses who, even with more hectic schedules, feel in control of their work lives. Robert Karasek of Columbia University has found that people with little control over their work, like cooks, garment stitchers, and assembly line workers, have higher rates of heart attacks than people who control the pace and style of their work. In Karasek's research, the highest risk groups for stress-related illness were those whose jobs ranked high in the demands made on them, but low in their control—jobs such as telephone operators, waiters, and cashiers. Their risk of heart disease was increased by about the same degree as cigarette smokers or those with high cholesterol levels.[6]

One way we can maintain our sense of control and reduce the stress in any situation is to look for the humor in it. With a sense of humor we view problems from a distance—in the big picture instead of with the incapacitating tunnel vision of fear and anger. We keep our cool and see beyond the here and now, and so we can think more objectively and clearly. We are not denying the problem, but we see it with enough perspective to realize

74

that it is not the end of the world. And remaining in control, we can act rather than just react.

In his book *Adaptation to Life*,[7] Dr. George Vaillant of Harvard Medical School analyzed a forty-year study of healthy men, showing that they are not people without challenges in their lives, but rather people who have developed mature methods of coping with challenges. Prominent among those coping techniques is a good sense of humor.

For challenging and potentially stressful situations, it's hard to beat wars, and so it's no accident that many people engage in humor in wartime. When the Nazis marched into Vienna, for example, they seized Sigmund Freud. Later they offered to let him leave the country, if he would sign a document saying that he had not been mistreated. Freud not only signed the paper they gave him, but added a note: "I can heartily recommend the Gestapo to anyone." The Nazis didn't get the joke, but it made Freud feel much better as he escaped their tyranny.

During Hitler's bombing of London, the city was plastered with signs on bombed shops proclaiming, "Open as usual." One shop that had barely one wall left standing sported the sign, "More open than usual." It was humor like this that kept the British sane and united in their will to defeat Hitler.

Such signs can be found after almost any disaster. When several neighborhoods burned in Santa Barbara, California, in 1988, one homeowner put up a sign outside the charred remains of his house—MY CHIMNEY'S BIGGER THAN YOUR CHIMNEY. During the 1993 flood in Des Moines, Iowa, someone put up this sign next to a flooded parking lot: NO FISHING.

As another example of humor reducing stress, consider the Iran hostage crisis of 1979. For many involved, being taken hostage was extremely stressful because they lost all sense of control over their lives. But one of the hostages maintained his feelings of control by saving a bit of food from each meal and putting it in his pocket. The next time one of his captors came to his cell, instead of sitting in the corner waiting to see what would *happen to him,* he got up, welcomed the person, introduced himself, and, holding out the piece of food, said, "Would you care for something to eat?" This playful restructuring of his role—from victim to host—changed his outlook and preserved his sense of control and dignity. In a situation where many became helpless victims, his sense of humor empowered him.

Father Lawrence Martin Jenco, who was a hostage in Lebanon, provided another example of the empowerment of humor. "Every night," Jenco said, "our captors would ask what they could get for us. They rarely fulfilled the simplest request. So soon we always responded in unison, 'A TAXI!'" This joking gave them the upper hand for a moment and also promoted their feelings of solidarity. Indeed, the joke was not wasted even on their captors. The night Jenco was released, one of them put some money into his hand and said softly, "Here's your five bucks for a taxi, now go home."

Jenco and his fellow hostages also maintained feelings of control by naming things. They called one of their standard meals "Hint of Chicken." "That meant," he explained, "that the chicken had quite recently walked through our rice."[8]

Another account of the value of humor in overcoming powerlessness is found in the book *Beyond Survival,* by Navy Captain Gerald Coffee, who was a prisoner of war in North Vietnam. After three months his jailor ordered him to wash in a rat-infested shower room littered with rotting bandages and garbage. What came out of the spigot was a trickle of cold water.

> And now here I was in this dismal, stinking hole, body broken, totally uncertain of my future . . . Men dying in adjacent cells, my crewman possibly dead . . . Finally I raised my head. And there at eye level on the wall in front of me, scratched indelibly by some other American who'd been there before me, were the words "Smile, you're on Candid Camera!"

Coffee "laughed out loud, enjoying not only the pure humor and incongruity of the situation, but also the beautiful guy who had mustered the moxie to rise above his own dejection and frustration and pain and guilt to inscribe a line of encouragement."[9]

And we don't have to be POWs or hostages to use humor to maintain our sense of control and relieve stress. At an engineering firm, the level of stress was high when a woman named Roe had an 8 lb. 3 oz. baby boy. A birth announcement went up on the bulletin board, but then someone added a piece of paper under it with "Name the Baby Contest" at the top. For the next few days people jotted down three dozen suggestions, including:

Zor Roe	Fidel Cast Roe	Tennisp Roe
Merrill Lynmon Roe	Skid Roe	Velk Roe
Beg Steelerbar Roe	Kiliminja Roe.[10]	

This playful exercise not only reduced the stress, but got people's creative juices going again.

Sometimes it's not just one person or office but a whole city that needs humor to relieve its stress. The winter of 1991-92 was especially severe for Syracuse, New York. By late winter, a record 162 inches of snow had fallen, and everyone was aching for spring. So at a meeting of the city council someone proposed, and the council unanimously passed, the following new law:

> Be it resolved, on behalf of the snow-weary citizens of the city of Syracuse, any further snowfall is expressly outlawed in the city of Syracuse until December 24, 1992.

Of course, this resolution did not give the people of Syracuse any real power over the weather, but the laughter it provided did block feelings of helplessness and keep them going for a few weeks until spring.

Many of the problems we face are like the weather—beyond our control—and often the best way to respond to them is to laugh. An extreme example comes from recent discoveries of asteroids and comets threatening our planet. In 1989, astronomers found an asteroid that passes close to Earth each year. It's about one-tenth the size of the asteroid that hit our planet 65 million years ago, sending up the dust clouds that killed off the dinosaurs. And sooner or later, it will collide with either Earth, the moon, or Mars. If it hits our planet, it will crash with the force of 20,000 one-megaton bombs. A few years ago, when this discovery was reported in the newspapers, many of them put humor in their stories, and several comedians worked this possible disaster into their routines. One editorial was titled: "The best protection: Root for Mars." More recently, the International Astronomical Union announced its discovery of a comet that could hit Earth with the force of 100 million atomic bombs, wiping out all of civilization. This would be the worst thing that ever happened to the human race, but again, many newspapers reported it with humor. One paper even had a cartoon of a comet with a nasty face swirling toward a frightened earth.

This humor about the worst possible catastrophes is healthy because there is nothing we can do about them. Fear and anger are helpful when they mobilize us to avoid danger or overcome an obstacle, but they are pointless and damaging when the danger is unavoidable. Then it's psychologically healthier to laugh than to get stressed out.

Pretend for a moment that scientists confirm that a passing comet is actually going to end life on this planet, say next Thursday. Would it be better to spend our last few days crying and bemoaning our fate, or laughing and having a good time? I'm sure that there would be lots of great jokes circulating about the Big One, and I for one would keep them going.

Laughing at what we cannot control is beneficial not just with global catastrophes, but with everyday problems. Suppose, for example, that someone you work with has an annoying habit of leaving dirty coffee cups in the sink. No matter how much you've complained, the person keeps on doing it. You could continue to get upset each time it happens, which will do you no good whatsoever, or you could face the inevitable with a sense of humor. In their book *Is It Worth Dying For?,* Robert Eliot and Dennis Breo suggest a way to handle problems like this. They call it the "Brain Tumor Technique." The next time the person, say, leaves a dirty cup in the sink, say to yourself, "Poor Dave has a brain tumor that makes him leave dirty cups in the sink. Fortunately, the tumor won't get any worse, but as long as he lives, he'll leave cups in the sink. I feel sorry for him."

Other Stress Reducers

We have seen how overcoming stress is largely overcoming feelings of being threatened and helpless, and we have shown how humor does this. But before leaving the topic of stress, it would be helpful to consider some other ways of reducing stress, many of which can be combined with humor.

1. **Stay healthy.** Eat right, get enough sleep, and get regular exercise. People who are sick, tired, and out of shape are more prone to stress. Speaking personally, when I am overtired and it has been weeks since I got any exercise, tiny problems bother me. When I'm well-rested and I've had a swim on my lunch hour, I'm not only more efficient but far less likely to become stressed out by even major problems. Exercise tones the muscles, works off nervous energy and calories, and keeps your heart and lungs healthy.

2. **Have people to support you.** Human beings are a social species; we need each other to cope with the strain of everyday problems. Indeed, there is strong evidence that friends and family play a vital role in keeping us healthy.[11] It is easier to feel threatened and helpless when you are alone, and so people who try to go it alone are more vulnerable to stress.

When you face stressful situations at work, talk about what's bothering you, with people at work and people at home. They may have useful suggestions, and even if they don't, just having them listen helps work off some of your tension.

3. **Recognize that there's no such thing as perfection.** Our reaction to any situation is based on our understanding of how things are supposed to happen. We feel frustrated and angry when the experience doesn't match these expectations. If we have unrealistic expectations, we are setting ourselves up for frustration, and so for stress.

One pattern of unrealistic expectation that causes untold stress is perfectionism. If I expect everything other people and I do to be perfect, then I leave no room for them or me to take risks, be creative, or learn from mistakes. The simple fact is that on earth there's no such thing as perfection. Is a 100-0 football game a perfect game? No—the score could have been higher. Is a report perfect when the boss says she likes it? No—it could have been completed in half the time. Perfect means that something could not have been any better, and nothing meets that criterion: *any* job could have been better. The best we can hope to achieve is continual improvement, not perfection.

Perfectionism actually hinders improvement, because it gets us so upset at mistakes that we don't learn from them. What if when we were children learning to walk and talk, our parents had screamed at us each time we fell down or mispronounced a word? We would have been so stressed out that we would have stopped trying. Fortunately, they were not perfectionists—they praised the part of what we were doing that worked, and they encouraged us to improve. And so we did.

81

The realistic person knows that nothing worth achieving is without mistakes and failures. For many seasons Babe Ruth led the league not only in home runs but in strikeouts.

4. **Recognize that you don't have to please everyone.** Another sure-fire way to generate stress is to have an excessive need for approval. If I feel like a failure every time someone is unhappy with me, I'm bound to be under constant stress. For unless I work with just a few of my very best friends, there will always be someone who doesn't like something about me or what I have done. In many situations a realistic expectation is that most people will approve of me most of the time. In other situations even that is too optimistic.

5. **Manage your time wisely.** One of the biggest sources of stress in the contemporary workplace is time pressure. Many jobs that can be done without stress and can actually be enjoyed—when we have enough time—turn into stressful jobs when we are rushed. And in most workplaces today, people are being given more to do in less time. If you are disorganized and work inefficiently, you'll be adding extra time pressure to your work, guaranteeing more stress.

Take on a reasonable amount of work, and learn to delegate when appropriate. Remember that a lot can be accomplished if you don't care who gets the credit.

When you are asked to do too much, or to do something in an unreasonably short time, tell the person making the request. This is especially important for women, who often accept more work than they can handle because they have been raised to nurture and help.

If you face a desktop full of work, divide it into piles and prioritize the tasks. Then divide the first big task into smaller tasks, and get to work.

6. **Seek balance between your work and the rest of your life.** You are more than your job. If you live just for your job, not only will the rest of your life be a shambles, but in time your work will suffer too. Workaholics may feel like they're getting a lot done, but studies have shown that they do not accomplish more than their colleagues who refresh themselves and enjoy their families and friends in their time away from work. And eventually the stress caused by overwork leads to exhaustion. As the title of a *Psychology Today* article put it, "All Work and No Play Isn't Even Good for Work."

For some people it's helpful to have a ritual to mark the end of the work day and the beginning of the rest of their day. In their book *Lighten Up*, C.W. Metcalf and Roma Felible describe a few. One vice-president of a large industrial plant takes the last five minutes of each work day to write down all the unfinished tasks that might follow him home and bother him until he gets back to the office. Then he puts this list in a desk drawer, locks it, and hangs up the key. Backing out of the office, he points at his desk and says loudly, "Stay!" A group of businesswomen keep red foam-rubber clown noses in their glove compartments. Each day as they head out of the parking lot for home, they put on their noses. Metcalf has his own draw-the-line ritual. He's bald, so hanging on the hat rack in his office he has a curly blond wig. As he leaves each day he puts on the wig to remind himself that the rest of his life is now beginning.[12]

And when you are home, here's a tip for adding hours to your day, and enriching your family life and personal happiness. Unless there is a particular TV program you're interested in, leave the television set off. Watching TV takes up 38 percent of our non-work time, more time by far than any other activity, and yet in survey after survey, people say that most television is a waste of their time. Indeed, those who watch the most TV often report feeling guilty; and when they are asked how much TV they watch, they report watching much less that they do, as if out of embarrassment.

Most television sets are turned on for the same number of hours each day, regardless of what programs are on. That's because most people turn on the TV not to watch particular programs, but just to have something to occupy their attention. Since the advent of cable TV and the hand-held channel-changer, most TV-watching is just "channel-surfing," flipping through the stations.

Many people say that they watch TV to relax, but TV brings a curious kind of relaxation quite different from exercising, making something, playing music, conversation, playing a game, reading, and other *activities*. While we are watching TV we are relaxed. In fact our bodies and brains are more passive than in any other state except dreamless sleep—even dreaming involves more brain activity than watching TV! But as soon as we turn the set off, we are no more relaxed than we were before we turned it on. Watching TV is only temporarily relaxing, and then only because it's so totally passive. It does not *refresh* us in the way *activities* do.

Try this: tonight skip TV and *do* something instead. See if you don't feel better when you go to bed and tomorrow when you wake up.

7. **Plan relaxation into your work time.** You should have periods of refreshment not just after work but during the work day. If you skip breaks and you work through your lunch hour, you may get more done

84

today, but you're creating stress and so hurting your mental health, physical health, and long-term productivity.

Books on stress reduction suggest dozens of exercises for relaxing in just a few minutes. Many of them involve clearing your head of all that's been filling it, a mental "minivacation," C.W. Metcalf calls it. Find a quiet spot where you can be alone for five minutes. Close your eyes and picture your favorite beach, mountain lake, desert vista, or other vacation spot. Feel the warmth or coolness. Hear the waves or the birds or the wind. Notice the smells of the place. Luxuriate in the feelings you get.

Some people find props helpful for taking these mental vacations. A saleswoman Metcalf knows carries in her briefcase a sachet of cedar chips she collected in a forest in British Columbia. To get in the mood, she just opens her briefcase and closes her eyes. For you it might be a few pebbles from your favorite beach, or even an audiotape that you can pop into your private tape player.

8. **Don't allow anyone to put you into an inferior position without your consent.** A basic cause of stress, as we've seen, is feeling that your power and control have been reduced. So if someone tries to threaten you or treat you unfairly, act assertively but reasonably to stop the person.

9. **Last, when you are feeling a lot of stress, find harmless ways to release it.** Take five deep breaths. Clench and unclench your fists, take a fast walk, or make wild faces at the boss's picture. There are several punching bags on the market that have suction cups on the bottom to attach to your desk. The Wham-it™ comes in sizes from a desk-top model to a six-footer, and features a clear plastic pocket at the top. "For

85

maximum relief," the instructions say, "insert a photo of the object of your disaffection in the plastic pocket. Then, pound and pummel to your heart's content. Comes with ideas for more extreme abuse." My own desk sports a $7.95 Radio Shack Executive Stress Eliminator. I couldn't resist the advertising: "Blast away at stressful situations with exciting sound effects. Six different sounds: zapper, rat-a-tat, laser shot, bombs away, quick-shot, and blaster . . . . Instead of clobbering your coworker or bashing your boss, zap 'em with a shot from the Executive Stress Eliminator." When I go back for new batteries, I think I'll pick up the automobile model for my car; it has even more sound effects, like "grenade launcher" and "death ray."

As you think up your own ways of getting rid of negative emotional energy, you'll probably come up with funny ideas such as these. And humor helps in several of the other stress-control techniques above, too, such as drawing the line between our work and the rest of our lives, and planning relaxation into our work time. Our sense of humor gets us to see ourselves and our problems more objectively, with less self-centered emotion, and with this more realistic perspective, we aren't tempted to expect perfection or total approval. Alone and with other stress-reduction techniques, humor offers us a way to get perspective on our lives and to maintain our feelings of control, so that we are not emotionally swept away by our problems.

In the middle of the last century, the American orator Henry Ward Beecher captured this value of humor nicely when he said that a person without a sense of humor "is like a wagon without springs—jolted by every pebble in the road." As you drive on your own rocky roads, remember to keep your humor springs in good repair.

WHAT'S GOOD ABOUT IT? A GROUP EXERCISE

Exercise 4-2

Take some situation or event that you would consider a disaster. Suppose this building's air conditioning system totally shut down while you were riding an elevator and then the elevator got stuck, so there was absolutely no ventilation. Now list ten ways that situation would benefit someone. For example, no one would have to get back to work. Everyone could compare the types of deodorants they use—and their efficacy! Get the idea?

Looking at disasters in this way relieves a lot of the stress. Often, disasters reveal the very best in people, prompting comments such as "disasters have their good side." And if disasters have their good side, then don't ordinary situations such as having to take a bus home or not getting a promotion?

LAUGHING AT FEAR. A GROUP EXERCISE

Exercise 4-3

Think of something that makes you feel afraid. Describe the object of your feelings, and the feelings themselves, in an exaggerated way. If you're afraid of public speaking, for example, describe the last group you talked to as a bunch of bloodthirsty vampires. As you share these funny descriptions with each other, you'll find that we're pretty much alike in our fears, and that laughing together about our negative feelings cuts them down to size. Other humor techniques are also useful in reducing fear. For fear of public speaking, take a look at Ron Hoff's *I Can See You Naked: A Fearless Guide to Making Great Presentations.*[13]

Notes

1. "Stress: Can We Cope?" *Time*, June 6, 1983, p. 48.

2. Ibid., p. 48

3. Steve Wilson, *The Art of Mixing Work and Play* (Columbus, OH: Applied Humor Systems, 1992), p. 33.

4. K.C. Corley and others, "Cardiac Responses Associated with 'Yoked Chair' Shock Avoidance in Squirrel Monkeys," *Psychophysiology*, 12 (1975), 439-444.

5. C.W. Metcalf and Roma Felible, *Lighten Up: Survival Skills for People under Pressure* (New York: Addison-Wesley, 1992), p. 96.

6. "Stress: Can We Cope?" *Time*, June 6, 1983, p. 52.

7. George Vaillant, *Adaptation to Life* (Boston: Little Brown, 1977).

8. C.W. Metcalf and Roma Felible, *Lighten Up: Survival Skills for People under Pressure* (New York: Addison-Wesley, 1992), pp. 103-104.

9. Ibid., p. 102.

10. Roger von Oech, *A Whack on the Side of the Head* (New York: Warner, 1990), pp. 96-97.

11. Patricia Wuertzer and Lucinda May, *Relax, Recover: Stress Management for Recovering People* (San Francisco: Hazelden, 1989).

12. C.W. Metcalf and Roma Felible, *Lighten Up: Survival Skills for People under Pressure* (New York: Addison-Wesley, 1992), pp. 161-164.

13. Ron Hoff, *I Can See You Naked: A Fearless Guide to Making Great Presentations* (Kansas City: Andrews and McMeel, 1988).

CHAPTER 5

HUMOR MAKES US MENTALLY FLEXIBLE

What Is Mental Flexibility?

In the last chapter we saw that keeping our sense of humor in a potentially stressful situation allows us to see the big picture and maintain our feeling of control. In this chapter we'll see a family of other valuable traits that humor fosters, a family I call "mental flexibility."

The essence of mental flexibility is the ability to handle different situations in different ways, especially to respond effectively to new, complex, and problematic situations. The mentally flexible person is able to:

- see things from several perspectives
- tolerate ambiguity and uncertainty
- take risks willingly
- adapt to change
- learn from mistakes
- solve problems in new ways
- switch between practical and non-practical thinking.

To understand the value of these abilities, it's useful to look at the opposite of mental flexibility, mental rigidity. If a bear sets out to swim across a lake and there are no obstacles, it will continue in a straight line until it reaches the other side. But if on the way, the bear encounters a floating log or other large obstacle, it turns around and swims back to where it began. Many people operate like that. They do all right in familiar situations in which everything goes as planned, but in new situations, or old situations with surprises, they are distressed. Faced with something unfamiliar, either they overlook its newness and treat it as a version of something familiar, or they recognize its newness and treat it as threatening. Whichever response they make, they do not adapt themselves to the new situation, and do not take advantage of the opportunities it offers.

Many people become more mentally rigid the older they get. Early in life they form a few concepts to categorize things and events, and they find a few ways to handle some basic situations. Then for the rest of their life they deal with every situation using only those concepts and techniques. Do you know anyone, for example, who threw tantrums as a child and found that the behavior worked to get his or her own way, and now as an adult yells and screams to achieve the same result? History provides many examples of mental rigidity in entire societies. Consider the launching of the first hydrogen balloon in 1783. When the unmanned balloon came down in the French town of Bonesse, the villagers were terrified. The men attacked it with pitchforks, hoes, and scythes. Hissing sounds and foul smells came from the holes they made, so they jumped on the balloon and ripped it to shreds. This balloon was something new to them, something which did not fit into any of their mental boxes. But instead of being stimulated to curiosity, wonder, or delight, they saw it as an invading monster.

Needless to say, none of them went on to invent the dirigible.

A century later when the automobile was invented, many people treated it as a threat. Hundreds of local laws were passed to limit the use of automobiles: some even required that a person with a lantern walk ahead of the vehicle. And even people who did not see the automobile as a menace tended to think of it as a version of something they already knew. Early cars were called "horseless carriages," and because horses go in front of carriages, the engine was placed in the front of the car.

Now no one is completely mentally rigid or completely mentally flexible, but the more flexible people are, the healthier they are mentally, while the more rigid they are, the closer they are to mental disorders. Sanity is largely appreciating the differences between situations, while mental disorders are responses that ignore differences. Paranoia, for instance, is indiscriminately responding to situations as threats.

It would be foolish to try to completely avoid seeing new situations as familiar ones, of course, for that's how any of us learns anything. But we do need to be on guard against getting into mental ruts in which we miss what is *new* about new situations. See Exercise 5-1 on the following page.

THE RUNNING TOTAL

Exercise 5-1

As a simple illustration of mental habits, use a pencil and piece of paper to do some simple addition. Write down each number as it is given to you, and then say aloud the total of all the numbers so far.

- The first number to write is 1,000.
- Under that write 40, then say the total aloud.
- Write 1,000 under that, then say the running total.
- Next write 30; say the total.
- Next write 1,000; say the total.
- Next write 20; say the total.
- Next write 1,000; say the total.
- Finally, write 10, and say the grand total.

Was your grand total 5,000? That's what most people get.

Your paper looks something like this:

```
    1,000
       40
    1,000
       30
    1,000
       20
    1,000
       10
  _____
    5,000
```

Exercise 5-1 (concluded)

If your total was 5,000, please go back over your last step, where you added 10 to 4,090. Most adults, including bankers and accountants who have tried this, add the numbers quickly and get 5,000. Most fifth-graders go slowly and get the right answer: 4,100. Why?

Well, we've done much more adding than kids have, so we get into patterns more easily. One pattern here is that we kept jumping to the next thousand. After doing that three times, we were ready to do it again, so it was easy to jump from 4,090 to 5,000, even though we were only adding 10. Had I simply asked you to add 4,090 and 10, you would have gotten the right answer.

There was another pattern here too: most adults say to themselves the words "One *thousand*, one *thousand* forty, two *thousand* forty, two *thousand* seventy," and so on. If we had to *say* the right answer—4,100—we would probably have said "forty-one *hundred*" (rather than "four *thousand* one hundred") and this would have broken our pattern. So instead we stayed in our mental rut and said "five *thousand*."

Even in our high-tech workplaces with their emphasis on speed and efficiency, we get into many counterproductive mental ruts. Consider the keyboard on our typewriters and computers, as illustrated below.

Did you ever wonder how it was designed? The layout of the keys is highly inefficient. Only 30 percent of the typing is done on the "home row"; only one vowel is on that row. The left hand, for most people the weaker, does 57 percent of the work, and the weakest fingers—the little fingers and the left ring finger—do a lot of the heavy work. Many familiar words and sequences of letters require the fingers to jump around between rows.[1] If you wanted to design an awkward layout for the keys, in fact, you couldn't make one much more awkward than our standard keyboard. In fact, according to one explanation, this awful arrangement *was* designed to reduce typing speed. When the Scholes company came out with its first typewriters in the 1860s, they received complaints about keys jamming. So they redesigned the keyboard, putting keys that were often hit in sequence, farther apart. Scholes didn't even think about overworking the weakest fingers, because he intended his machine for two-fingered typing.

In 1912 a film study of typists showed how inefficient the standard keyboard is, and in 1936 August Dvorak patented a much more efficient one. As you can see from the illustration above, it puts all the vowels on the home row. Most of the typing—70 percent instead of 30 percent—is done on the home row. The right hand does 56 percent of the work, and the strongest fingers get the heavy work. One study showed that while the fingers of a fast typist cover twelve to twenty miles per day with the standard keyboard, they cover only one mile with the Dvorak keyboard.

Today few typewriters and no computers have keys that *can* jam, most typists use all ten fingers, and the Dvorak keyboard has been available for over half a century. But we have kept Scholes' inefficient keyboard anyway. Good evidence of our mental rigidity here is that few of us have even *considered that* our keyboard might be improved. We simply learn to use it and then put up with it for the rest of our lives.

Allied with the force of habit to produce mental rigidity, is our strong tendency to follow authority figures and large groups. As many social scientists have shown, human beings want someone to tell them what to do. That's why democracy has been so rare throughout history, and why even in democracies we tend to leave practically all the decision making to our leaders.

Many of the routines on the old *Candid Camera* TV program showed us our natural conformism. In one, several people from *Candid Camera* took over an empty elevator and faced the back wall instead of the door. As unsuspecting people got onto the elevator, they too faced the back wall. In another routine, a sign was placed on a wall next to a sidewalk. It said "WALK BACKWARD ZONE" and several shills walked backward as they reached the sign. Seeing them obeying the sign, many passersby did too. Another stunt had a group of *Candid Camera* staff sitting in a doctor's waiting room in their underwear. As regular patients came in for appointments, many of them obligingly stripped down to their underwear.

Today's Workplace Calls for Mental Flexibility

Now on *Candid Camera*, conformism simply made people look silly. In our work, it makes us act mechanically rather than flexibly. Unfortunately, many traditional workplaces taught workers to be mentally rigid and simply follow procedures. Consider factories that divided large jobs into the smallest, most mindless tasks possible, and asked workers to repeat those tasks, like robots, hundreds or thousands of times a day. A person's forty-year career might consist of putting bolts into car doors! In such a job, performing tasks from sheer habit was not only encouraged, it was considered a virtue.

But now the old-fashioned jobs—production, service, clerical—in which workers simply repeated a number of predetermined steps for eight hours a day, are fast disappearing. And while fifty years ago people could start working at one job and count on retiring from that same job, today over 12 percent of us are retrained each year, and no one has the job security which was the norm just a few years ago.

In our highly competitive postindustrial economy, where nothing is certain and rapid change is the rule, we can no longer afford mentally rigid workers. Business as usual, as many companies have discovered in the last few years, can easily put you out of business. Traditional mindless jobs are now being taken over by robots and computers, and the jobs that are left require people to learn new skills quickly, think on their feet, and work smoothly with other people. In short, we need mentally flexible workers.

Humor and Mental Flexibility

In bringing mental flexibility to our workplaces, humor can help a great deal. To understand how humor promotes flexibility, recall our discussion of the Incongruity Theory in Chapter 2. Humor is enjoying something that violates our mental patterns. But as we saw, humor is not our only reaction to incongruity. Sometimes when things don't happen as we expect, we get frightened or angry. In order to laugh about a situation rather than be upset by it, we have to step back from it and see from a higher, less engaged perspective. But this distanced perspective and looser attitude of humor is also characteristic of creative problem-solving, risk-taking, and other traits of mental flexibility. The mind-set of humor, that is, is the mind-set of mental flexibility.

Humor fosters mental flexibility in two main ways. First, it blocks the negative emotions of fear and anger that make us act rigidly. And second, it gets us to see things from several perspectives, and from unusual perspectives.

Humor Blocks Negative Emotions

In Chapter 2, we saw that whether we experience some surprising event as upsetting or as amusing depends on whether we see it with mental distance. We are emotionally overcome by problems when they seem right on top of us and they fill our attention. When we laugh about something, on the other hand, we are not obsessed by it, it does not seem right on top of us, and we are not overcome by negative emotions.

By blocking negative emotions, we block the accompanying mental rigidity. The emotions of fear and anger, as we have seen, evolved in early animals as quick automatic responses to danger. No complex mental processing had to occur. In humans, too, these basic emotions don't involve much thinking. When we're overcome by fear or anger, we seldom come up with great ideas, or even new ideas. We just act out of habit. Have you ever been in the middle of an angry argument and suddenly stopped screaming to announce that you had just thought of a great solution to the problem that started the argument? Probably not. Anger and fear tend to shut down our higher thinking processes; they do not bring out creativity or even clear thought. That's why we speak of "blind rage."

The loss of control we feel in fear and anger is not just over our situation, but also over ourselves. Negative emotions are not so much things *we do* as things that *happen to us*. They are *reactive* rather than *proactive*. That's why we describe ourselves as overtaken by these emotions, and after a bout of anger, we say, "I don't know what came over me."

When we want to remain in control and be mentally flexible, in and out of the workplace, negative emotions need to be eliminated. And here humor is invaluable. One place where we see humor used to block negative emotions is in medicine. Nurses and doctors often face stressful situations where negative emotions might overpower them and render them unable to think clearly. So to stay cool-headed, rational, and flexible, they sometimes joke about those situations. Recall the story in Chapter 2 of the doctor reviving the man with the bullet hole over his heart, by cutting him open, reaching into his chest, covering the hole, and squeezing his heart. To react to such a crisis in a totally engaged way, with emotions like anxiety and fear, would be to freeze. But by seeing what is going on with enough distance to joke about it, medical staff stay cool and can exercise their skills. This, in fact, was the basic theme of *M*A*S*H*, one of the most successful TV sitcoms of all time.

Disgust is another emotion that medical people have to repress in order to stay flexible. As Vera Robinson, R.N., explains in her book, *Humor and the Health Professions*, medical humor is "often raunchy, sensual, scatological, aggressive and 'gallows,' that is, macabre, black, gross," but that's because in medicine "we are dealing with illness, naked bodies, blood, guts, excrement, trauma and death!"[2] One way nurses and doctors block disgust is by making up funny names for potentially disgusting things. "Floogers," for instance, is medical slang for chunks of mucus coughed from tracheotomy openings (probably a contraction of "flying" and "booger"). "Code brown" means feces found in an inappropriate place like a hallway or bed.

Not only medical staff but also patients use humor to keep their cool. A hospital chaplain in Oregon told me of a patient being prepared for surgery who asked the technician for three inches of rubber tubing. The technician gave it to him and then left the room. A few minutes later a student nurse came in to give the man his pre-surgery enema. When she had all the equipment in place, she asked him, "Does that seem OK?" He rolled his head, looking up at her with the rubber tube sticking out from between his teeth, and said, "I think that's far enough." She dropped everything and ran out of the room.

Because humor blocks negative emotions and keeps people mentally flexible in stressful situations, we look for humor in our leaders. We want people who will see things in perspective and not be overcome by anger, depression, and other emotions.

Abraham Lincoln was perhaps this country's greatest president largely because he stayed clear-headed and mentally flexible through the worst five years in this country's history, as 360,000 Americans were killed, not by foreign invaders but by fellow Americans. He stayed in emotional control by keeping his sense of humor. When he was criticized for joking at a cabinet meeting, Lincoln replied, "Gentlemen, why don't you laugh? With the fearful strain that is upon me night and day, if I did not laugh I should die, and you need this medicine as much as I do."

Business leaders, too, lead more effectively when they show a sense of humor, especially about themselves. In

1980 when Lee Iacocca was dealing with Chrysler Motors' huge financial problems, he reduced his own salary to $1 a year. Getting lots of questions about this decision, he called his top management together and said, "Don't worry, I'll spend it *very carefully.*" Suddenly there was no longer a problem! With this quip Iacocca had shown that he saw situations coolly and rationally and he was in control.

In Chapter 8 we'll explore more connections between humor and leadership, but now let's turn to the other basic way in which humor promotes mental flexibility—by giving us multiple perspectives on situations.

Humor Gets Us to Shift Our Perspective

Mentally flexible people avoid mental ruts; they notice and take advantage of what is new and different in each situation. So they have to be able to shift their point of view easily. All this is closely connected to humor, for in appreciating and in creating humor, we see things one way and then suddenly see them another way.

In jokes, as we saw in Chapter 2, we are led along one mental path, but then at the punch line we shift to another. In hearing Mae West's quip "Marriage is a great institution, but I'm not ready for an institution," we at first understand "institution" to mean a set of social customs, but then switch to a very different meaning—mental asylum.

Another technique of humor is to look at something familiar from an unfamiliar perspective. When McDonald's came out with its breakfast menu featuring the Egg McMuffin, for example, Jay Leno commented, "Oh great, before I could only eat two meals a day in my car." Or consider Charles Kurault's comment on our high-speed national highways: "Thanks to our Interstate Highway system, it's now possible to drive from Maine to California and not see anything." Both Leno and Kurault took what was touted as an advantage and presented it as a disadvantage. What we call wit is this ability to flip ideas around, and look at things from new angles.

In flipping ideas around, we can go from negative to positive as well as the other way. Kenneth Littleton Crow is a comic who is also a paraplegic. In talking about his disability he says, "There are advantages to being in a wheelchair, though. Wherever you go you have a seat, and a pair of shoes will last you twenty years."

It is the ability of humor to get people to see things in new ways that makes it so powerful as a device of persuasion. Consider this letter to the editor, written in early 1992, during the national debate about whether gays should be allowed in the military.

Should heteros serve?

The inspector general's report on the disgraceful and obscene behavior by Navy personnel at the 1991 Tailhook convention brings up a fundamental question that the Defense Department ought to address: Should the present policy which allows heterosexuals to serve in the Navy be changed?

Reprinted courtesy of the Gannett Rochester Newspapers

To test your own mental flexibility, try two exercises, one with words and the other with a picture.

The first is from Dr. Joel Goodman of The Humor Project. Read the sentence below:

WOMAN WITHOUT HER

MAN IS NOTHING.

How did you group the words? One possibility is:

[A] woman without her man is nothing.

Another way is:

Woman—without her, man is nothing.

Can you switch back and forth between these two meanings?

Now, look at the drawing below. What is it?

Did you say a bird? A rabbit? A pair of scissors? The OK sign? Even if you saw the drawing in just one way at first, are you now able to see it in these other ways too? If you are, then—as with the ambiguous sentence above—you are comfortable with things that can be interpreted in more than one way. You have a tolerance for ambiguity.

Many people have low tolerances for ambiguity. I once showed the bird-rabbit picture in a seminar for division managers of a large company. When I asked what it was, the highest-ranking male in the group answered immediately, "It's a bird." Then someone else said, "A rabbit." To which the first man snapped, "No, it's a *bird.*"

Unfortunately, American business has too many managers like that, who want each thing or situation to have one interpretation, each problem to have one solution, and each moment to come under one set of rules. Although they may work hard and show loyalty to their organizations, they get entrenched in certain ways of thinking and acting, without considering other ways that might work better. Suspicious of anything new or ambiguous, they put the brakes on innovation.

In psychological tests, such people show a preference for familiarity, definiteness, regularity and symmetry. Often they think in opposites, categorizing everything as either black or white, good or bad, conservative or liberal, etc. These polar categories make their thinking easy, of course, but at the expense of detail, subtlety, and accuracy. Needless to say, these people have little sense of humor.

Try another little test. Can you locate yourself on this map?

This is not the way we have been taught to think of the Americas, of course. It's natural to think, "But North America is *up*, South America is *down*." But that's only our mental habit. North can just as easily be down, and south up. In the 19th century, for example, the area around Toronto was called "Upper Canada." If we were Martians flying toward Earth, it would be just as natural to view it as in the drawing above as it would be to view it in the standard way.

Laughing at Yourself

Although humor and mental flexibility are important generally, they are most important when focused on yourself and what happens to you. The basic ability here is to see yourself from the outside—as the old *Candid Camera* jingle put it, to "see yourself as other people do." Will Rogers said that everything is funny if it happens to the other person. That's an exaggeration, but it contains the truth that while it's easy to enjoy incongruities in other people's lives, it's harder to enjoy them in your own. If at lunch your friend spills a bullet-hole-shaped blob of ketchup on his shirt, you'll probably be able to laugh. But what if you spill a similar blob on your own shirt? You'll see the humor here only if you can see yourself objectively, from the outside, as you saw your friend.

When I make breakfast I'm usually about half awake. More than once, I've done something like this: pour the cornflakes into the bowl, go over to the stove for the coffee pot, come back to the table and start pouring coffee onto the cereal. When I realize what I'm doing, I have a choice. I can stay locked in my original perspective of making breakfast; realize that I have wasted coffee, cornflakes, and time; and get angry. Or I can step outside my perspective of breakfast-making, see myself the way a neighbor might see me through the kitchen window, and laugh.

I'm proud of the fact that about 50 percent of the time when things like that happen, I'm able to laugh; and I'm trying to improve that percentage. Not just because laughter feels better than stress, but because laughing at myself gets me out of my own head. Instead of seeing myself as the center of the universe, I see myself more realistically as just another human being among billions, any of whom might have made the blunder I just made. In laughing at myself, I'm really laughing at human nature, and that's liberating.

Another recent example of laughing at myself was my first attempt at skiing last January. My wife, an expert skiier, took me. Assessing my athletic aptitude pretty well, she dropped me off at the "Bunny Slope." For the next two hours I followed gravity in all kinds of ways, a few of them actually involving my skiis gliding over snow. A lot of the time I was on my back. Five- and six-year-olds scooted around me shouting, "Get out of the way." By the end of the morning I could do the basic moves, and in the afternoon I made good progress on the adult beginners' slopes. Along the way I looked pretty silly, but so what? As the kids laughed at my slips and falls, I laughed along with them. I simply had not invested my ego in my skiing.

I wish that I could drop my ego that easily while driving. When another driver changes lanes without signalling, I usually take that as showing personal disrespect for *me*. When someone honks, they must be singling *me* out for personal criticism. Somehow in traffic I become the center of the universe, and take offense at almost anything. One thought that has helped me loosen up behind the wheel is this line from comedian George Carlin: "Did you ever notice when you're driving how everyone going slower than you is a moron, and everyone going faster than you is a maniac?" As soon as I acknowledge this thought, that *I* am the only one going at exactly the right speed, I realize that every other driver thinks the same thing. What I am laughing at here is the way the human mind is set up to give itself all kinds of special consideration. And in laughing, I stop giving myself special consideration and see myself as just another driver. See Exercise 5-2 on the following page.

FOREHEAD SIGNATURE

Exercise 5-2

Here's a little exercise to test your ability to laugh at yourself. I want you to do something you've done thousands of times, only in a different way. Take a pad, or a piece of paper folded over, place it against your forehead, and sign your name as you would sign a check.

How did you do? If you're like most people, you failed. But you were probably able to laugh, or at least not be upset.

How could you find your failure funny? Well, this is an unusual task. It's not a common skill, and certainly not part of your job. So when you failed, it was not at anything you considered essential to your self. Your self-esteem wasn't threatened, and so you could look at your mangled signature with distance and objectivity.

Wouldn't it be wonderful if we could see all our mistakes and failures this objectively? We have no trouble seeing clearly what our colleagues, boss, and subordinates do incorrectly. But when we look at our own performance, we give ourselves extra points. Often, indeed, while judging others by their actions, we judge ourselves by our intentions, interpreting what we have done so that it wasn't a mistake after all.

If we learned to laugh at ourselves more, we would have a more objective and constructive attitude toward our mistakes and failures.

By way of confessing mistakes and failures, I should admit that when I started doing my seminars I didn't use the forehead signature exercise to illustrate these ideas about laughing at oneself. Instead, I designed an exercise that turned out to be threatening to many people: I asked them to take out their drivers' licenses and exchange them with the people sitting next to them. My point was that almost everybody looks bad in the photo on his or her driver's license. I asked, in fact, "How do those photographers at the DMV get jobs taking these awful pictures?" I showed a blown-up version of my license photo in which my eyes are closed and mouth open, and I look hungover. But even this joking about myself was not able to get several people to laugh about their license photos. At one seminar, at least a third of the participants became non-participants as soon as I asked them to exchange drivers' licenses. The whole exercise bombed.

My poor judgment wasn't the only thing wrong here. These people who quickly stuffed their licenses back into their wallets and purses had a problem too: their ego circles were too large. "Ego circle" is my term for all the features people have that put them on the defensive and that they are not willing to look at objectively. To have a sense of humor about yourself, you need to shrink your ego circle, so that you look at yourself in the way you look at other people.

The best person I ever worked for, Peter, had an ego circle the size of a pencil point. He was the head of two group homes, one for teenagers, where I worked, and the other for ten mentally retarded adults. At the end of the week he would visit the second house to hand out small checks to the retarded adults, and they would head off to the bank to cash them. One Friday, after distributing the checks, Peter remembered that he had a small agency check of his own to cash, so he followed the group to the bank. He waited in line, handed the teller his check, and received his cash. He counted it out loud, "Twenty, thirty, thirty-one, thirty-two, thirty-three." The teller looked him straight in the eye and with a big smile said, "Very *good*, Peter, very, very *good*!"

Many people in that situation would feel insulted and threatened. Their response would be something like, "Do you have any idea who I *am*?" But not Peter. He had no trouble shifting his perspective to see himself the way the teller did—as the eleventh retarded person in the line—and that sudden shift made him laugh so hard that he fell on the floor. He didn't have to run to the bathroom, but he certainly made a spectacle of himself. And then he couldn't wait to get back to tell us what had happened— to him, the Administrator!

Few management textbooks even mention humor, but some of those warn managers against looking foolish in front of their subordinates. They will lose respect for you, the standard advice runs. Peter showed that this advice is 180 degrees wrong. Not only did we not lose respect for him when he told us what had happened in the bank, but we had even more respect for him.

Thinking of Peter's episode in the bank calls to mind Robert Frost's short prayer:

Forgive, O Lord, my little jokes on thee.
And I'll forgive thy great big one on me.

Here we can connect humor not only with mental flexibility but with self-esteem.[3] If you feel good about yourself, you are more likely to be able to laugh about what happens to you. When things don't go as you expected, you can remain calm and not get defensive, instead of being overcome by fear or anger. And seeing situations with a sense of humor, you are not only calmer but more objective and able to see more possibilities.

Insecure people who lack self-esteem, by contrast, tend to be humorless and narrow in their vision. Feeling threatened by every setback, they tend to react in pre-set, mentally rigid ways. They also tend to judge their own value as persons by every task they perform. With their egos constantly on the line, they need to succeed at everything. In severe cases of low self-esteem, no amount of success changes their negative picture of themselves, they see humor in nothing, and nothing makes them happy.

People with a good sense of humor, on the other hand, have more realistic and flexible standards for evaluating themselves. They can accept imperfections in themselves and in others as part of the human condition. While humorless people think of themselves as far inferior to their ideal self, people with a good sense of humor estimate themselves to be fairly close to their ideal self. That allows them to be more content with their lives. Those with low self-esteem see a big discrepancy between their real self and their ideal self, and are likely to suffer stress and depression.

Humor and Creativity

So far in talking about mental flexibility, we have concentated on relatively passive forms of flexibility. But mental flexibility also includes active abilities—to put ideas together in new ways, to solve problems, and to engage in other forms of creative thinking. Here, too, humor goes hand in hand with mental flexibility.

Many books on creativity have stressed its connection with humor. Arthur Koestler, in *The Act of Creation,*[4] showed how the process of bringing together ideas from different realms, which he calls bisociation, operates in scientific discovery, in artistic invention, and in creating humor. Edward deBono, today's foremost authority on creativity, has written that "Humor is by far the most significant behavior of the human brain. ...Humor... shows how perceptions set up in one way can suddenly be reconfigured in another way. This is the essence of creativity."[5]

Although it has been a hot topic for decades, creativity is still widely misunderstood. Contrary to popular misconceptions, creative people do not have higher IQs than the rest of us. Nor is creativity a special talent like musical ability or physical coordination. Rather it is largely an attitude toward our work and our life as a whole. It is a way of organizing our experience, our thinking, and our activity.

Creative people are playful, experimental, and willing to take risks. In facing a problem, they're likely to try indirect rather than head-on approaches. Creative solutions, and creative ideas generally, seldom emerge when we are concentrating on something in a solemn, practical mood; they are more likely to come when we are in a relaxed, even playful mood.

What were you doing the last time you had a great idea? If you're like most people, you were taking a shower, driving, brushing your teeth, or even sleeping. And you probably weren't *confronting* a problem with a solemn, head-on attitude. More than likely you were batting ideas around and making lots of connections, perhaps funny connections, between them. You were playing as much as working.

Notice that the features of creativity mentioned so far—playfulness, experimentation, and risk-taking— are prominent in a group of people who don't get much serious attention: young children. Creativity consultants now charge thousands of dollars to show people how to put ideas together in creative ways, something young children do all the time. Indeed, cultivating our own creativity is largely recapturing the attitudes we had as kids.

I once took a three-year-old to a carnival, where she spotted a cotton-candy vendor. "I want that," she called out. "*What* do you want, Amanda?" I asked. "Ice cream fur!" she said.

Here was someone who had been speaking for only a year inventing a new name for cotton candy as easily as you or I would think of the old name. In fact, I like "ice cream fur" better—it describes the bottom cone part as well as the fuzzy top part.

With their more open attitude, young children see connections between things that adults tend to miss. For my son Jordan's fourth birthday we got him a Venus Fly-trap, the carnivorous plant with the spiked pods that close on insects. A few days later he was rummaging through a drawer in the bathroom and found a hairclip of my wife's, with spring-loaded sides and teeth that looked like his new plant. Squeezing it open, he came running up to me. "Daddy, Daddy, wanna play Venus Fly-trap? You be the fly!"

As adults we are conditioned to think of each thing as having one name and one use. If I came into your office squeezing a hair-clip and asking you to play Venus Fly-trap, you'd probably call the Security department. With our playfulness suppressed and our thinking narrowed, is it any wonder that we have to hire consultants to get us into the frame of mind which we had most of the time when we were young children?

Divergent vs. Convergent Thinking

For many of us it was formal education that suppressed our natural playfulness. It was probably in school that you first heard that our goal in life was to "do good work," and that play, laughter, and other forms of "fooling around" were incompatible with good work. Teachers often suppress humor not only because they see it as disruptive, but because it represents a kind of thinking that they don't know how to handle—divergent thinking.

Schools specialize in convergent thinking— using memory and logical thinking to reach the single right answer to a question or problem. In divergent thinking, by contrast, there is no single right answer. One exercise in divergent thinking, for example, has these instructions:

Think of 30 improvements for the standard bathtub/shower. Cost and technical feasibility are no object. There are no wrong answers.

In most school assignments, students have to focus on one narrow issue, and not let their mental train be sidetracked. Above all, they have to monitor what they say or write, to avoid making any mistakes. But in this assignment there's no possibility of making a mistake, so you can let ideas flow freely. And it helps to let one thought lead to lots of only slightly connected thoughts. Traditional schools avoided this kind of thinking. Of the thousands of exercises and exams you had through your education, how many were anything like the one above? How many made your thinking spread out rather than focus tightly? How many stimulated your imagination?

Roger von Oech, in *A Whack on the Side of the Head*,[6] tells of a revealing experience he had one day in tenth-grade English class. His teacher picked up the chalk and put a dot on the blackboard. "What is this?" she asked. Having been raised with the standard view that each question has one answer, and not wanting to get the wrong answer, the students were reluctant to say anything, but finally someone got the courage to say, "A chalk dot on the blackboard." The other students, relieved that someone had given the correct answer, had nothing to add. Then the teacher told them how she had done the same exercise the day before in a kindergarten class, and they had come up with fifty answers: an owl's eye, a cigar butt, a star, the top of a telephone pole, etc. For these five-year-olds without school experience, the world was a big amazing place where they could see all kinds of connections between things. With ten years of formal education, the best the high school students could come up with was "A chalk dot on the blackboard." With whatever they had gained in knowledge in those ten years, they had lost a good deal, too, in imagination, playfulness, and spontaneity.

Now the convergent thinking taught in schools is important: we need to know facts and be able to think logically about them. But when convergent thinking is all that students are exposed to, their thinking is severely restricted and their creativity squelched.

If we think of education as a preparation for life, then we have to cultivate divergent as well as convergent thinking in students. How many times at work, or in your family life, after all, are we faced with problems which have just one right answer? When was the last time at work that the challenge before you was anything like a multiple-choice test?

Humor and Divergent Thinking

The connection between divergent thinking and humor is a strong one. Humor loosens up our minds and gets us to put ideas together in new and usual ways. Dr. Alice Isen found that people who had just seen a funny movie showed more creative flexibility in solving problems than a similar group who had seen a serious movie. Dr. Avner Ziv found that students who had enjoyed a comedy recording scored higher on a test of divergent thinking; and people who had engaged in humor *actively*, by thinking up captions for cartoons, scored even higher. And that's just what we should expect if the experts are right that creating humor is itself a kind of creativity.

118

In generating creative ideas, it's natural and useful to come up with odd, even outlandish ideas. In fact, one of the guiding principles of brainstorming is that the wilder the ideas, the better. When a brainstorming group is laughing, that's a good sign. In a group in which I once participated, for example, the task was to think of twenty-five uses for a three-ounce paper cup. As often happens in brainstorming, our first dozen ideas were pretty ordinary. But then, as we got loosened up, the ideas got funny and creative. Number 17 was "Hat for a parrot"; number 21 was "deposit envelope at a sperm bank." (For numbers 22-25, send me a stamped, self-addressed envelope.)

Now some creative ideas are funny without also being useful, but funny ideas often turn out to be very useful. If we look over the history of inventions, almost all new ideas seemed funny at first. Today as we sit down to dinner, for instance, we take it for granted that we will use forks. But a few centuries ago when the fork was first used, it was considered outlandish. Indeed, its use was forbidden in the British navy until the late 19th century. Vaccination, the motor car, the airplane, and countless other inventions were also thought funny when they first appeared.

Even when funny ideas are not put to use as is, they can lead to useful ideas. Practical ideas can "piggy-back" on wacky ideas. Consider the paint company where a group of engineers was discussing the difficulty of removing old housepaint in preparation for repainting. One engineer said, "Why don't we add gunpowder to our paint? Then you could simply blow the old paint off the house." That idea got some laughs and they did not implement it. But it led them to develop a way of "blowing the old paint off"—they put an additive in housepaint that made it fall off the house when a special liquid was sprayed onto it.

At a dog food company, the brainstorming centered around the possibility of non-digestible additives in the dog food. One person suggested flower seeds, so that dog "nuisances" on the lawn would at least lead to flowers. Another person suggested a non-toxic, glow-in-the-dark dye, so that at night joggers and walkers could avoid stepping into a mess. Neither of these ideas was implemented as is, but they led to the addition of grass seed to cattle feed, to re-seed Western rangelands; and to glow-in-the-dark salt licks for wildlife.

Many, maybe most, great inventions have come from similar divergent thinking. While on a fishing trip in northern Canada, Clarence Birdseye noticed a pile of fish an Eskimo had frozen in ice; that led to his invention of frozen food. In 1948, the Swiss chemist and mountaineer George de Mestral was peeling burrs from his socks when he got the idea for Velcro®. Dozens of other products came from similar happy accidents—corn flakes, Ivory® Soap, vulcanized rubber, Rayon®, the microwave oven, the Sony Walkman®, Teflon®, skateboards, kitty litter, Scotchgard®, artificial sweetener, and Post-It® notes.[7] What are Post-It® notes, after all, but slips of paper with a weak adhesive on the back. Viewed from a conventional perspective, that adhesive was a failure. But the person who developed Post-It® notes had the imagination to see its usefulness.

Reframing

One way in which humor promotes divergent thinking is by "reframing" situations, or restructuring the elements of the situation into new patterns. Reframing is a standard technique of jokes and other humor. Consider the sign in front of the store: "We buy old junk. We sell antiques." Or the remodeling tip: "The best way to add a room to your home is to have one of the kids move out."

The way we structure the elements of a situation can make a huge difference in how we approach it. Some years ago a poll was taken in Switzerland asking, "Do you think it's OK to smoke while you're praying?" Almost 90 percent of the respondents said, "No." A similar group was asked, "Do you think it's OK to pray while you're smoking?" Over 90 percent of this group answered, "Yes"!

Lots of problems become more manageable with a little reframing. Several years ago as a young assistant professor, I had an annoying, blustery senior colleague who at first drove me up the wall. But one afternoon as he stormed into my office unannounced, I suddenly pictured him as "Yosemite Sam," the loud-mouthed Warner Brothers cartoon character whom Bugs Bunny laughs off. Suddenly it was easy to tolerate the guy. Since that experience, I've used this technique often. Try it yourself: picture the bore next to you on the long jet flight as Elmer Fudd, the vain woman at the party as Miss Piggy, etc.

Problems can even be solved with reframing. During a New York City garbage collectors' strike in the 1970s, people had to devise new ways of getting rid of their garbage. One man wrapped his garbage each night in gift wrapping paper with a colorful bow, and then put it on the front seat of his unlocked car. Each morning the garbage was gone.

In the final weeks before Disneyland opened in 1955, Walt Disney was running out of money to finish the landscaping. The plants that had been put in had little signs with their Latin botanical names on them. So Disney told the landscaping crew to look up the Latin names for the weeds that hadn't been cleared, and put them on little signs in front of the weeds. Disneyland opened, and nobody noticed anything wrong with the landscaping.

American Airlines was losing money on its late night flights, the so-called "red-eye specials," until it reframed these flights as "Midnight Specials." The airline served champagne and played music, turning these flights into parties. Business went up 70 percent.

As another example of reframing in marketing, consider contemporary wheelchairs. Until fairly recently, wheelchairs were seen as just transportation for people who couldn't walk. And so they all looked functional and dull. But then someone started thinking of wheelchairs as a different kind of transportation—in the same category as motorcycles and cars. So they developed models like "Wildcat" and "Turbo" that came in colors and had racing stripes. Indeed, now people race wheelchairs.

Dropping Restrictive Assumptions

Another way humor helps in creative thinking, especially in problem-solving, is by challenging our assumptions. The December when my son was five years old, he announced that he was going to chop down a Christmas tree for us in the woods near our home. Unfortunately, the evergreens in these woods were thin and scrawny, and we traditionally get nice, full Christmas trees that hold lots of ornaments. As the problem set up in my head, it was an insoluble dilemma—*either* we got the kind of tree we wanted and broke Jordan's heart, *or* we let Jordan cut a pathetic tree for us and we endured it through New Year's. My wife and I talked about this dilemma late into the night. Suddenly she laughed. "Why don't we get the tree we want *and* let Jordan cut it down?" she said. Her plan was devious. While she took Jordan sledding, I went to the tree lot and got the kind of tree we like. I took it into the woods near our house, nailed two crossed pieces of wood to its base, set it up among the trees near the main trail, and covered the crossed sticks with snow. When she and Jordan returned from sledding, she suggested to him that this would be a good time to chop down our Christmas tree. He put on his lumberjack shirt, got his ax, and we all hiked into the woods, where with a few nudges he found the beautiful Christmas tree and chopped it down.

In the 1960s Jean-Claude Killy challenged the assumptions of ski racing to become the greatest skier ever. Instead of keeping his legs together, as was standard, he skied with them apart, for better balance. And instead of leaning forward when he came to a turn, he sat back on his skis, which "jetted" him through the turn. His new unconventional style of skiing, which has since become known as the French style, won him three gold medals in the 1968 Olympics, as well as the World Cup.[8] The lesson to be learned from Killy is that often you will be more successful not by accepting the traditional assumptions of the game and trying harder, but by questioning those assumptions and reinventing the game.

Here's another kind of success that came from dropping an assumption, this one from the newspaper column
"Hints from Heloise." A beauty parlor owner was tired of
bending over to pick up hairpins from the floor. But as
long as she assumed that someone had to pick them up,
she couldn't see an easier way to do it. Then one day as
she watched her dachshund Trudy walking around the
shop, she dropped that assumption. She hung magnets
from Trudy's collar, which automatically picked up the
hairpins.

Or consider the manager at Xerox who found that the
supposedly quick informational staff meetings he scheduled for first thing Monday mornings were getting longer
and longer. The assumption he dropped was that they
would sit down for the meeting. Standing, no one felt the
need to keep talking. They simply exchanged updates
and went back to their work, which was exactly what he
had wanted all along. "Vertical meetings" have been used
with similar success at Equitable Life Assurance, Corning
Inc., and Johnson & Johnson.

From the beginning of cable television, cable companies have faced the problem of people tapping into their
service without paying for it. But finding out who they
were and securing hard evidence against them was
difficult. As long as cable companies assumed that they
would have to do expensive detective work to catch
these culprits, they were reluctant to go after them. But
recently some companies have dropped that assumption,
and gotten the culprits to announce themselves, sending
in evidence of their guilt at the same time. These companies broadcast a "special unbelievable offer" for something like a free trip to Florida, only they block that

broadcast from reaching the homes of their paid subscribers. When people write in to claim their free trip, they have thereby incriminated themselves, and have even signed the evidence! The company simply turns over their letters to the police.

If we can profit this much from questioning one or two assumptions, what might happen if we questioned large numbers of assumptions? One company that found out is Hewlett-Packard. In designing the new assembly line at its Roseville plant, it "started out by wiping the slate clean," according to Max Davis, manufacturing manager of the plant. The company questioned not just this or that aspect of the plant, but everything. Over two and a half years, Hewlett-Packard completely overhauled the way it built everything. As a result, costs for raw materials have been cut by 50 percent, paperwork has been reduced 90 percent, and labor time 75 percent. The computer terminals made by the new plant cost from 5 percent to 45 percent less than those made overseas. And product reliability is much higher than before—only 4 percent of the work force is now needed for repair work, compared to 20 percent for computer terminals made the old way.[9]

Fostering a Constructive Attitude toward Mistakes

In problem-solving and other creative processes, humor has another benefit, too—the tolerant attitude it fosters toward mistakes and failure. As Ross Perot said, mistakes are like skinned knees for kids. "They're painful, but they heal quickly, and they're learning experiences."[10] And in getting back up after you skin your knees, nothing is more helpful than your ability to laugh at what happened.

Any creative work is a high-risk, low-return venture. For every success, there will be lots of unworkable ideas and false starts. Today the average millionaire entrepreneur has gone bankrupt three times.[11] Thomas Edison, the Wright Brothers, and most other famous innovators failed many more times than they succeeded. They are remembered only because they learned from their mistakes and kept going.

Most people know that Edison invented the light bulb; few realize that it took him 10,000 tries before he hit on the combination of a carbon filament in a partial vacuum surrounded by glass. Developing his storage battery took Edison almost 25,000 tries, and he had over a thousand other patents! Is it any wonder that he was always ready to laugh at himself? "When down in the mouth," he wrote in the margin of one of his notebooks, "remember Jonah—he came out all right." Had Edison lacked a sense of humor and treated every failure as a crisis, he would not have been able to even begin his projects.

Whatever your work, if you want to achieve anything creative, you have to treat mistakes as part of the process. They are not things to be shunned or covered up, but things to be embraced and learned from. As Thomas Watson, Jr. of IBM once quipped, "The way to succeed is to double your failure rate." Robert Townsend in *Further Up the Organization* put it more strongly: "Admit your own mistakes openly, maybe even joyfully."[12]

Having a constructive attitude toward mistakes makes you not only better at creative work generally, but more effective in working with other people. If you can laugh at your own mistakes, you'll be more tolerant of others' mistakes and more supportive of them. We'll see more about this and other social benefits of humor in the next chapter.

Notes

[1] "A Better Way to Type 'The Quick Brown . . .,' *Discover*, August 1986, p. 10.

[2] Vera Robinson, R.N., Ed.D., *Humor and the Health Professions*, 2nd ed. (Thorofare, NJ: Slack, 1991), p. xix.

[3] Rod A. Martin and others, "Humor, coping with stress, self-concept, and psychological well-being," *Humor: International Journal of Humor Research*, 6 (1993), pp.89-104.

[4] Arthur Koestler, *The Act of Creation* (London: Hutchinson, 1964).

[5] Edward deBono, *Serious Creativity* (New York: Harper Business, 1993), p. 8.

[6] Roger von Oech, *A Whack on the Side of the Head*, 2nd ed. (New York: Warner, 1990), p. 24.

[7] Robert Kriegel, *If it ain't broke . . . BREAK IT!* (New York: Warner, 1991), pp. 155, 156, 213.

[8] Ibid, p. 103.

[9] *San Francisco Chronicle,* Nov. 9, 1987, C1, C7.

[10] *Inc.* January 1989, p. 60.

[11] Robert Kriegel, *If it ain't broke . . . BREAK IT!,* (New York: Warner, 1991), p. 193.

[12] Robert Townsend, *Further Up the Organization* (New York: Harper and Row, 1984), p. 141.

CHAPTER 6

LAUGHTER AS SOCIAL LUBRICANT

Humor Brings Us Together

So far we have concentrated on the values of humor for individuals. But to appreciate humor fully we need to look at it as something we experience together, and create for each other.

It's rare that we laugh when we're by ourselves, but we laugh easily in groups. In fact, laughter is contagious. If we approach a laughing group, we usually start laughing before we find out what they're laughing about. There have even been laughter epidemics. One of the best documented started at a Catholic girls' high school in East Africa in the 1960s. When the girls went home, their laughter spread to their mothers and sisters. Over a thousand "victims" were affected, many collapsing from exhaustion after laughing for several days.[1]

Why do we laugh together easily? Several scientists have suggested that laughter developed in early humans as a way of establishing, strengthening, and smoothing out social relationships. As a species, we are dependent on one other, but at the same time we tend to get in each others' way and even threaten each other. Humor and laughter bring us together and reduce the natural friction between us.

Smiling and laughing are among the oldest and most powerful social gestures human beings have. As any parent knows, the baby's first smile, and a few months later the first laugh, are milestones in the parent-child relationship. In children's and adults' relationships, too, the first laugh we share with a person raises the level of acceptance and trust. As Victor Borge put it, laughter is the shortest distance between two people.

When you want to get to know someone, one of the first things you do is make them smile or laugh. On meeting new people, it's natural to create rapport with a funny comment about the weather or the traffic. In fact, humor may be the single most important way we have of establishing and maintaining intimacy.

A second grade teacher in one of my seminars told me of a writing assignment in which she asked her students to describe the kind of person they wanted to marry. One girl wrote simply: "I want to marry someone who can make me laugh without tickling me."

When a publishing company tallied the characteristics most frequently mentioned in the personal ads of its newsletters, "Sense of humor" topped both the men's and the women's lists. In a survey of 350 brides-to-be asking what they admired most in their men, sense of humor was mentioned most often, outranking romantic nature, good looks, and intelligence. Another study of 351 couples married 15 years or more, found that the most admired qualities in a spouse were a sense of humor, integrity, caring, and sensitivity.[2] Public speakers know the power of humor to establish rapport; that's why they so often begin presentations with humor. I recently heard a long talk by a man who had moved to the U.S. from

Spain. He opened with these two sentences: "Though I have lived here for over twenty years, I still have a considerable accent. At first it may cause you trouble, but by the end of my talk you will find it charming." Presto! Everyone laughed, sympathizing with him and wanting him to do well. So his accent, which without the humor might have bothered us, very quickly *did* sound charming.

If you observe a group of people, say at a restaurant table, who go half an hour without laughing, I'd give you odds that they are not close. And I'd stick to my bet even if they have come together to discuss something very serious, like a big business deal or plans for a funeral.

Indeed, it is often precisely when situations are the most serious that we need humor to break through the formality and establish a human connection. A woman from one of my seminars told me that when her mother died, she had to make the funeral arrangements. Sitting in the funeral director's office, she asked him, "Do you mind if I smoke?" "That's fine," he answered, "most of my customers smoked." Now humor is not something we usually associate with funeral directors, but in this case it created instant rapport.

It's because humor flows naturally among people who feel close that we suppress it when we do not feel close. If my wife and I are in the middle of an argument and our young son comes downstairs with his pants on backward, we will go out of our way to avoid laughing, because that would show that we're getting back together.

In the workplace, the value of humor cannot be overestimated. Studies have shown that if you smile, you are

131

more likely to be hired for a job, and are more likely to be trusted once in that job. Creating effective work groups is largely a matter of creating effective communication between people, and humor, as we'll see, enhances all kinds of communication.

Most workplaces and most professions have funny stories and jokes that promote solidarity among members of that group. I call this their humor lore, and when you take a new position, you don't feel part of the group until you're in on some of this lore.

Sharing humor builds morale, camaraderie, and team-spirit, and the mental flexibility it promotes is indispensible in groups working together. One way humor promotes good morale is by giving us a way to "blow off steam," to complain without bitching. Good morale in an organization is not a lack of complaints—in every workplace today there's plenty to complain about. Rather, good morale is an open atmosphere in which complaints can be expressed and they are listened to. Where management allows humorous griping, there is much less of an "Us against Them" attitude. If people are allowed to joke about problems, morale can stay high even when nothing can be done right away about those problems.

Here I need to return to a point from Chapter 2—that humor is not the same as joy or optimism. Indeed, when everything around you is falling apart, nothing is less funny, except unintentionally, than seeing that yellow "Have a nice day" happy-face. Unqualified optimism is unrealistic and often annoying.

But humor does not have to be optimistic to improve morale. It can even *emphasize* the negative side of things. Consider the bank where morale was at an all-time low.[3] The tellers didn't get along with each other, and no one liked the customers. The manager didn't handle the low morale by passing out happy-face buttons or giving phony pep-talks. Instead he faced the problem realistically and with humor. He started a "Worst Customer of the Week Contest." On Friday afternoons the tellers got together to present their horror stories; the winner got a certificate and a bottle of champagne. The tellers loved the contest. They laughed through each others' stories, but as they laughed they started appreciating the difficulties their colleagues faced. That increased their sympathy with one other, creating camaraderie. And because the tellers wanted to win the champagne, they started looking for the really bad customers. If they saw an alien life form wandering around the bank, they'd smile and say pleasantly, "I can take you over here, sir! How may I help you?" As they became nicer to the customers, of course, the customers became nicer to them. In a matter of weeks the bank's morale problem was over.

Given the connection between humor and morale, it's no surprise to learn that there's a correlation between the amount of humor and fun shared in a work group and its cooperation and productivity. As Henry Donaghy, CEO of Donaghy Financial Services, puts it, "Fun forges cooperation quicker than any other human dynamic (other than catastrophe), and business today will live or die on how much team effort they can pump into every single production step they take."[4] See Exercise 6-1 on the following page.

HUMOR AMONG COLLEAGUES

Exercise 6-1

Close your eyes. Think of the people with whom you work most smoothly and productively. Open your eyes. Now close them again and think of the colleagues with whom you share humor the most often. Were the two groups almost identical?

Now close your eyes once more and think of the people you find it hardest to work with. Open your eyes. Now close them and think of the people with whom you seldom or never share humor. If you're like most people, there's a lot of overlap between these two groups, too.

Humor and fun also create good feelings with customers. In June 1994, Saturn held a "Homecoming Hoedown" at the Tennessee factory where Saturn cars are made. Along with factory tours there was entertainment— live country music and dancing, and food tents. In the midst of the fun, 30,000 strangers became "Saturn family members."

Even the federal government now figures in the "fun factor." A few weeks ago, after finishing my income tax return on the last possible day, I drove to the main post office to get it postmarked. Of course, I joined several hundred fellow taxpayers in the lines. To reduce the stress level here, one Postal Service worker taking envelopes from drivers was dressed as Uncle Sam and two others as clowns. The other last-minute tax filers that I saw appreciated this whimsy as much as I did, and in laughing together, the hundreds of us felt camaraderie.

Humor Gets Our Attention

One reason humor brings us together is that we pay attention to people who make us laugh, and we tend to like them. Funny people make us follow their train of thought, and their agenda. That's why humor is used so much in persuasion, especially advertising. Estimates of the number of television commercials that use humor range as high as 42 percent.[5] One marketing researcher studied 113 TV ads which had won International CLIO awards over a three-year period, and found that 69 percent of them used humor.[6]

Even negative messages can get favorable attention when they are funny. Consider the classic "Joe Isuzu" car ad. Or a restaurant sign I passed recently near Syracuse, New York:

CROSSROADS RESTAURANT

WARM BEER LOUSY FOOD

Of the hundreds of truckstops I've driven past, this was one of the few I wanted to stop at.

There are many other places for humor as an attention-grabber. Here's how one airline got people to pay attention to the pre-flight demonstration of the safety equipment. As the flight attendant started the demonstration, the voice over the speaker said,

> Good morning, ladies and gentlemen. Welcome to Flight 417. For those of you who haven't been in a car since 1952, we will now demonstrate how to buckle your seat belt. . . . In case of a loss of cabin pressure, oxygen masks will come down automatically. If you're traveling with a small child, put your own mask on first, and then their mask, if they've been good.

Another airline used this announcement at the end of a long flight across the Pacific, to get passengers to pay attention to the evaluation forms:

> Ladies and gentlemen, would you please fill out the evaluation forms your flight attendants are passing out. If you liked your flight, this is Air New Zealand Flight 256. If you didn't, it's Qantas Flight 1904.

Humor: The Gentle Persuader

Not only does humor get people's attention, but the unexpected delight which it brings relaxes them and puts them in a good mood. And that makes them more receptive to your message. As Regina Barreca says, "If you can make people laugh with you, you have won them over, however briefly, to your side. You have created an atmosphere of consensus, a moment of agreement when everyone is in sync."[7]

One place to find humor used as a gentle persuader is the personal ads section of newspapers and magazines. Here's one from *The Nation*:

> EMERGING CRO-MAGNON, 63, hunting
> upright female. No flakers. No swingers.
> Prehensile a plus. . . .

Think of how much more relaxed you would feel replying to this than to most personal ads. The man is obviously intelligent, but he doesn't take himself seriously. In billing himself as a caveman making progress, he pokes fun at himself, which makes him approachable. In fact I'd guess that in most readers' minds, his humor about himself would override his past as a primitive male. Humor even goes a long way toward overriding someone's present shortcomings, as in this ad placed in a Concord, California newspaper:

> TOTALLY INSENSITIVE MAN looking for
> totally uncaring woman for meaningless
> relationship... .

The man was swamped with replies.

A participant in one of my seminars told how she had made use of humor when she received a letter from the IRS notifying her that she owed an additional $350 in taxes. Many people would have responded to that letter by confronting it head-on, poring over their tax records to disprove the claims of the IRS. But that response is threatening to the IRS—it calls its competence into question. This woman had a different tactic—to persuade the IRS that as a grandmother living on a tight budget, she couldn't pay any more taxes. After calling the IRS for an appointment, she showed up carrying a glass with her toothbrush and toothpaste in it. Over her shoulder was a neatly folded towel. When the IRS agent asked her to sit down, she thanked him and politely placed the glass and towel on his desk. Smiling, he asked why she had brought these items. "Well," she said, "if I have to pay you $350, I won't be able to pay my rent and I'll have to move in here with you folks." Within ten minutes she left the office, back in the good graces of the IRS, having had to write a check for only $45. And I'm sure that she had made the agent's day.

Using humor as a gentle persuader can work even better if the humor is directed against yourself. Then you are not at all threatening to the other person, so he or she can relax and simply listen to your message. When male wolves are fighting and one wants to concede, it makes itself totally vulnerable by lying on its back and exposing its throat. The other wolf could kill it in a second, but never does. Instead, it simply accepts the victory and walks away. Poking fun at yourself can work the same way. The other person laughs along with you at your self-criticism, and then is freed of the necessity to criticize you any further.

When George Deukmejian was Attorney General of California, there was a complex case which everyone wanted more time to research. The judge was reluctant. Deputy Attorney General Asher Rubin asked for an additional sixty days. The judge snapped, "I don't give *anybody* sixty days. What the hell do you people in the Attorney General's office do all day?" Rubin answered, "Well, we spend most of our time trying to spell 'Deukmejian.'" The judge laughed and gave Rubin forty-five days more.[8] Because humor reduces people's defensiveness and at the same time delights them, many sales teams are now trained in creating humor and a sense of fun. An example is Target Stores, a national chain with over 450 stores in more than thirty states.[9] Starting in 1988, Nancy Robbins, head of Management and Organizational Development, offered humor training programs to salespeople and managers. In the first three years, more than 10,000 employees requested and completed some humor training. In customer satisfaction surveys, the number of positive comments has steadily increased and the number of negative comments steadily decreased. And there has been a steady decline in employee turnover since the program began.

Training and Educating

Another situation in which humor gets people to relax and receive your message better is training and teaching. Each year corporate America spends $200 billion training its employees. That is roughly equal to what's spent on high school and college education in this country. IBM alone spends $900 million to educate and train employees—more than the annual budget of Harvard University! But a lot of training and teaching isn't as effective as it could be, because the learners aren't in the right frame of mind. Here is where humor can help.

Because of early experiences with teachers who humiliate children for making mistakes, most adults are uncomfortable when put in the role of student. They feel like they're back in second grade, and their main motive is not the positive desire to learn, but the negative desire not to make any mistakes. So instead of diving into the material, taking risks, and really learning, they tighten up, ask no questions, don't answer unless they are called on, and generally just try to get through the class without being embarrassed. Obviously, that's not the right mindset for learning.

The stage of our lives when we learn the fastest is precisely the stage when we take the most risks and are least afraid of mistakes—our first five years. If we want to maximize our learning after that, we need to recapture the undauntedness we had as preschoolers. And humor can be a big help in setting a tone of acceptance of mistakes.

Right at the beginning of the course, the instructor should cite several examples of mistakes made by beginners. Last summer I took a course in glassblowing, which the instructor started by showing us some small, clunky, misshappen glasses made by beginning students. "We're here to make lots of lumpy shotglasses like these," he said with a smile. "If you finish the course having made two or three as good as these, you should be happy." We all relaxed and were ready to learn glassblowing.

Even better than simply showing students' mistakes is for instructors themselves to make a mistake in the classroom and laugh at it, or to tell a story of some mistake they've made and laugh at it. If they can't remember one, they can borrow someone else's mistake, or make one up and tell it as their own. The purpose is to show students that everyone makes mistakes, trial and error are part of learning, and there's no need to be defensive.

In my university teaching I often start off the first lecture in Logic by asking the students "Is this Intro to Logic?" They smile and say yes, and then I explain that I once walked into a classroom the first day and started my opening lecture on logic. A few minutes into it, the students looked confused and some started leaving the room. Finally one asked the question uppermost in all their minds, "Is this *Art History*?" In my haste to get to class, I had misread the room number, and the professor was late for the Art History class scheduled for the room I had commandeered. This was a pretty big mistake, and I describe it as a standup comic would. Students laugh at my story and can tell from it that I'm approachable and don't have a big ego. So they are able to relax and learn right from the beginning.

My wife also teaches—international studies—and last year in a class discussion of the Berber people of North Africa, a student asked if the Berbers weren't the ones who did such-and-such. "Yes," she answered, "at least that's true for the *rural* Berbers. But the *urban* Berbers..." As soon as the sounds "URBAN BERBERS" came out of her mouth, the students started to chuckle. Instead of repressing her own laughter, she let it out. She even flicked her index finger up and down through her lips fast, repeating "urban Berbers" several times. By exaggerating and laughing about the funny sounds she had produced, she got the students to relax, and so more were willing to get into the discussion. A more serious verbal slip she made recently was a spoonerism, a reversal of the beginnings of two words. In distinguishing the Kurds who live in Iraq from those who live in Turkey, she accidentally called the latter group the "Kurkish Turds." After the laughter died down, of course, she apologized to any students who might be of Turkish or Kurdish descent.

One area where humor is used extensively to promote a constructive attitude toward mistakes is computer training. Many adults, especially those well-along in their careers, feel anxious about having to learn computer skills. What if they make a mistake that their sixth grader wouldn't make? To get them to feel at ease, many training books and even computer programs use humor as part of their "user friendliness." Several poke fun at computer experts as "nerds." New Riders Publishing offers four computer guides called the *Non-Nerds* series. Que Publishers offers books with titles beginning "I Hate" followed by the name of the system being taught. This series uses characters from Jeff MacNelly's popular *Shoe* cartoons to illustrate sections and chapters. The Professor explains buzzwords; nerdy Skyler offers user tips. For those who don't mind admitting they're computer novices, there's *The Complete Idiot's Guide* series from Alpha Books, marketed as PC guides "for people with better things to do." The display materials for the series feature pictures of the character Cliff Claven from the TV sitcom *Cheers*. All of these books allow people to feel comfortable about their ignorance and the mistakes they will make, and so to get on with learning.

John Cleese, of the British comedy group *Monty
Python's Flying Circus*, the TV series *Fawlty Towers*, and
several movies, has built the world's largest production
company for training films on the simple insight that
when we bring mistakes out in the open and laugh at
them, we can reduce our natural defensiveness and learn
from those mistakes. Video Arts Ltd., which he founded
in 1973, now grosses over $20 million annually with its
120 training films, most of which are comedies. Cleese
explains that his films show trainees that "everyone all
over the world is screwing up the same way."[10] And once
you see yourself as just another person making a common mistake, it's much easier to correct that mistake.
The training film *Meetings, Bloody Meetings*, for example, shows what happens when a meeting has no set
agenda, people are allowed to arrive any time, the chair
doesn't cut off irrelevant side discussions, and on and on.
We've all made some of these mistakes, but ordinarily we
might not be willing to own up to them. When they are
all piled up in the film, however, we laugh, and in laughing we can admit, "Yeah, I did that last week." Then we'll
be more effective at our next meeting. This is training by
contrast—you learn how to do something by seeing how
not to do it.

Announcing Bad News

Ernie Kovaks once said, "If you're going to tell 'em
the truth, make 'em laugh or they'll kill you." That's an
exaggeration, but it contains the insight that people often
treat the bearers of bad news as if they were responsible
for what that news is about. In ancient Greece, military
couriers bringing word of a defeat were sometimes put to
death. We have milder punishments for people like

Walter Mondale, who as presidential candidate in 1984 pointed out the obvious: that the federal deficit was growing at an alarming rate and taxes might have to be increased to correct the problem. The American people didn't execute Mondale—they simply swept Ronald Reagan, a lifelong avoider of bad news, back into office by a landslide.

Confusing the news with the bearer of the news works with good news as well. By telling Americans what they wanted to hear, Reagan made us feel good, and thereby became the most popular president in recent memory.

Making people laugh is one way of making them feel good, and so people who deliver news—good or bad—with a touch of humor, make themselves more likable. Humor enhances the positive effect of good news and softens the negative effect of bad news. So when you bring good news, and especially when you bring bad news, put some humor into the delivery. If you're partly or wholly responsible for the situation being announced, you should probably make it self-effacing humor, which will both make the news easier to take and soften criticism of you. As we said earlier, if you have just criticized yourself, others are less likely to jump on you.

At a faculty meeting announcing budget cuts, my university's vice president for finance began with two stories making fun of the accountant-types that now dominate universities. The first was about a vice president addressing the faculty on increasing their productivity. A professor of violin raised his hand and asked, "What do you want me to do—play faster?" His second, more pointed story, was about an administrator talking to the faculty on how to compute the dollar value of various people's time, and the critic raised her hand to say, "You've done some impressive research. You know the cost of everything and the value of nothing."

By telling these stories before announcing the budget cuts, the vice president voiced the feelings of many professors, and thus forestalled their saying the same thing. The negative impact of his bad news was softened, and instead of spending the meeting expressing resentment, faculty members started thinking of concrete suggestions for reducing costs while preserving what was valuable in the budget.

Not long after that meeting, while rumors were flying about where our university budget would be cut next, the chair of my division circulated this memo:

Subject: New Travel Policy

Due to budget cutbacks, there have been several changes in the Travel Policy. They are as follows.

Transportation

- Hitchhiking in lieu of commercial transport is strongly encouraged. Upon receipt of a deposit, the University will issue a luminescent vest prior to departure on University business. Bus transportation will be used only in case of a tight schedule.

- Use of a personal automobile is authorized only if bicycling is clearly impractical. Reimbursement will cover only actual gas consumption, not mileage, and then only on downhill trips.

- Airline travel will be approved only under extenuating circumstances. Faculty are encouraged to cut costs by wearing a red cap and handling baggage for other passengers. Also the University will make available at cost small plastic roses for selling near a departure gate.

Lodging

- All employees engaged in travel are encouraged to stay with friends and relatives, and to make use of public parks and campgrounds, or bus terminals, train stations, and office lobbies.

Meals

- Expenditures for meals must be kept to an absolute minimum. Certain grocery stores provide free samples of promotional items. Travelers should also familiarize themselves with indigenous roots and berries.

- If restaurants must be utilized, travelers should seek out "All you can eat" salad bars.

Conference Registration Fees

- The University will not bear costs associated with conference fees. A generic "Hello, My Name Is . . ." sticker will usually suffice.

Apologizing

Closely related to bringing bad news is apologizing. And here too humor can reduce negative feelings, let people relax, and make them sympathetic to your position. A secretary accidentally drops the telephone, and retrieves it saying to the caller, "You're on Candid Telephone!" By not getting flustered or embarrassed or making excuses, she maintains her poise and control of the situation, getting the caller what was requested and delighting the person at the same time.[11]

146

One hot summer day I was taking a plane from New York's LaGuardia Airport. A problem in the airport's radar system had slowed down everything. After we had boarded the plane, it stayed at the gate for almost two hours, with no air conditioning. Everyone was soon fed up with the captain's frequent announcements—every ten minutes—of a new delay. In fact I was considering a mutiny myself. When the clearance for take-off finally came, the captain came on the PA. He could have simply apologized in a serious way, but instead he apologized and then said, "Now would you please return to your seats, so I can see out the rear-view mirror to back this thing out." That simple touch of whimsy made us drop our resentment and relax for the flight.

A few years ago the division I worked in had one secretary for two dozen professors. Donna tried to be cheerful under the workload, but often people gave her work with an unrealistically short deadline. At noon one day as I was leaving my office, lunch bag in hand, I noticed something on my desk that I had forgotten to give Donna for processing that morning. As I picked it up, I found something underneath that should have gone out the day before. So on my way to lunch I headed toward her office, wondering how I could apologize for making her rush. To make matters worse, as I approached her desk, I noticed lots of other work piled in front of her. "Donna, I'm sorry this is late; but could you get it out right away?" I began, handing her one form and simultaneously reaching into my lunch bag for my apple and Fig Newtons. "And could you get this other form out by five o'clock?" I watched her face tightening up. "And with your other hand," I continued, holding out the items from my lunch, "could you juggle this apple and these Fig Newtons?" She relaxed, laughed, and said "Sure, if you'll push my car home—it's low on gas!" Now we both laughed. Implicit in my juggling request, of course, was the admission that I was acting like a jerk, along with the promise that I wouldn't repeat this stunt. And I haven't.

While passing through Skaneateles, New York, on a Saturday afternoon last summer, my wife and I found another example of humor in apologizing. Asking around about a good place to eat, we were steered to Doug's Fish Fry. Walking through the narrow door we found a skinny old building crowded with people waiting for their orders. The fish looked good and the portions were big, but the space and the cooking equipment were clearly inadequate for the dozens of customers. In fact it took us twenty-two minutes to get our order. Used to instant Whoppers and Big Macs, we would have gotten impatient with the slow service—except for the sign on the wall:

> WE PROMISE TO SERVE YOU IN 5 MINUTES,
> OR 8 OR 9, OR HAVE ANOTHER BEER AND RELAX—
> IT CAN'T BE TOO MUCH LONGER.

That sign made all the difference. Instead of standing around anxiously watching the clock, we sat down at a table with another couple, ordered a round of beers, struck up a conversation, and enjoyed ourselves while waiting for our delicious fish.

When an apology comes with humor, the people who have been offended get something unexpected—a moment of delight just as they were starting to feel indignant or sorry for themselves. Instead of dwelling on what went wrong, they actually feel better. And that allows everyone to pick themselves up, dust themselves off, and keep going. That is usually healthier than a heavy apology which focuses on the offense and tries to explain the extenuating circumstances in detail. Would it have done any good, after all, for the airline captain at LaGuardia to go into detail about the series of delays? Or for me to tell Donna just how busy I had been that morning? In both cases, laughing together worked much better to restore the relationship.

Apologizing with humor also helps to restore the relationship quickly, by not making the person apologizing go into a subservient position from which he or she then has to reestablish equality. In laughing together, the two parties remain equals. Consider an apology of Louis Armstrong, the great jazz trumpeter. In the 1930s he had a contract with a record company which did not allow him to make records for anyone else. One afternoon the owner of the company was listening to a record on another label, and heard the distinctive sound of Armstrong's horn. He immediately called Louis in for a meeting. Armstrong sat down and the man played the record, without saying a word. When it was finished, Louis smiled and said, "That's not me, and I'll never do it again." Both laughed, understanding each other perfectly and ready to resume their friendly relationship.

Handling Unreasonable Complaints

Another situation in which humor can reduce tension is in handling unreasonable complaints. At a four-table restaurant near Syracuse, New York, many people ask to be seated by the window because of the lovely view. But since there is only one window and one table by it, their chances of sitting near the window are only 25 percent. After years of dealing with people grumbling at not being seated by the window, the restaurant adopted a new strategy. From the local builder's supply the owners bought three windows. They put sturdy frames around them and attached casters to the bottoms. Now when someone is seated near a wall and complains, "We wanted to sit by the window," the server smiles, goes into the back room, wheels out a window, and positions it next to their table. Almost all the customers laugh and drop their complaint.

In a nursing home one patient found fault with everything. At lunchtime one day, she called the dietician to her room. "This is a terrible, terrible lunch," she said. The dietician nodded. "This is a bad potato," she continued. Knowing that simply disagreeing with the woman would start a pointless argument, she tried a different tack. Picking up the potato with her left hand, she spanked it with her right, saying, "Bad potato, bad bad potato!" No one could remember the last time the old woman had even smiled, but when the dietician spanked the potato, she laughed out loud. After that she didn't complain about the food, and for weeks she shared the funny story with other residents.

Commanding and Warning

Adults, and most kids, do not like to be given direct orders. That's why we have so many polite, roundabout ways of telling people to do and not do things. Instead of commands, we make "requests." Instead of ordering someone to "Finish the report and bring it to me by noon," we ask a question, "Do you think you could have the report finished for me by noon?" Even when we offer someone something, we often add polite "if"-phrases just to show that we're not forcing them to take it. Instead of, "You can get more envelopes from the black cabinet," we say, "*If you want more envelopes*, there are some in the black cabinet." Even our word "please" is short for "if it pleases you." Linguists have studied sentences like these in great detail, showing how we go to considerable trouble to respect people's freedom and to avoid making them feel pushed around.

One of the most effective ways to make a command or warning not sound pushy is to add humor to it. In the summer of 1994, the Alaska Department of Transportation tried a new system for flagging motorists at road construction sites. Instead of having human beings holding up stop signs, they used robotic gorillas in hardhats and luminescent vests. Drivers are usually annoyed at being stopped by construction workers, but they loved the gorillas. Many even came back later with their cameras.

And consider this memo which a Milwaukee factory sends its workers a few days before the opening of baseball season:

> Any employee desiring to be present at the death or funeral of a relative, please notify the foreman before 10 AM the day of the game.

Although the humor in commands and warnings is often friendly, it doesn't have to be. It can even be playfully hostile. I was recently in Toronto for a presentation at a hospital. As I drove around looking for somewhere to park, I spotted what looked like a perfect spot just a block away from the hospital. Racing into the space, I looked up at the sign in front of me:

DON'T EVEN THINK OF PARKING HERE. IF THERE ISN'T
A BIG GREEN TOW TRUCK ACROSS
THE STREET NOW, THERE WILL BE SHORTLY.

Whoever chose that sign had to make drivers understand that they shouldn't park there under any conditions, and so the gentle reminder approach would not be appropriate. But he or she also wanted to avoid sounding like a bully. Their solution was a sign that made a threat so exaggerated that it was funny.

Here's another sign—to keep customers out of the work area of an auto repair shop:

LABOR RATES

REGULAR	$40 AN HOUR
IF YOU WAIT	$45 AN HOUR
IF YOU WATCH	$60 AN HOUR
IF YOU HELP	$75 AN HOUR

Evaluating and Criticizing

Perhaps even more than warnings, criticisms tend to make people tighten up and get defensive. If you're my boss and we're going over my annual performance evaluation, I may have the deepest respect for your authority and judgment. I may also like you as a person. But as soon as you start criticizing me, I'll tend to stiffen up and not listen objectively. And so I won't take your criticisms constructively.

The commonly heard suggestion "Don't take this personally" is right, but almost no one is able to follow it just through an act of will power. What I need is some

152

technique to see myself objectively. Here humor is invaluable. If you are sharing humor with me, you show that you're in a basically good mood, and are not out to "rake me over the coals." And where the humor focuses on the mistakes I have made, it helps me to see them without getting defensive.

The objective way for me to listen to your criticisms is to hear them as criticisms of certain *kinds of behavior*, not as criticisms of *me*. I need to look at myself as I look at other people, as just another person among billions. Humor gets me to see myself in this way, from the outside, and so helps me to remain calm, realize what I have been doing wrong, and correct it.

Here's a scenario: In a warehouse one worker—call him Bob—had been late without good reason several times over a two-week period. One morning at 9:15, when he was late again, the boss announced a contest. He offered $10 from his own pocket to the person who could most closely estimate the time of Bob's arrival. On a clipboard everyone signed up next to a time, and when Bob showed up an hour later, they all cheered as the prizewinner was announced. After that, Bob wasn't late any more.

Another way to get people to accept criticism objectively is to exaggerate the mistake until it becomes funny. Around 1980, Chase-Manhattan Bank in New York began putting this principle to work in dealing with often-repeated mistakes by tellers. Familiar ways of handling mistakes, like reprimanding people in the boss' office and sending them a critical memo, usually make them feel uncomfortable and defensive. What Chase-Manhattan did, instead, was have graphic artists make funny posters of the mistakes and the problems they caused. The posters were put up around the banks; the tellers saw them and laughed. Because they didn't feel threatened or uncomfortable, they could recognize their own mistakes in these posters. In over 95 percent of the cases where these posters have been used, the mistakes have stopped almost immediately.

Handling Conflict

Humor, we have seen, smooths out interactions in which one or both sides might feel uncomfortable. And its lubricating power is not limited to minor sources of friction—it works even when there is outright disagreement or conflict.

In a sixth-grade classroom the students were not getting along with the teacher. To step up the conflict, they had conspired to drop their books on the floor at precisely 10:15. At the designated moment, as the teacher was writing on the blackboard, dozens of books hit the floor. Many teachers would treat that as the opening volley in a battle, and go into a confrontational mode, shouting, trying to find ringleaders, and meting out punishments. But a reaction like that would have stiffened the students' opposition to her, and would have shut down learning for quite a while. This teacher responded differently: she quickly stepped over to her desk, collected her books into a pile, held them at waist level, and dropped them on the floor. "Sorry," she said with a smile, "I'm running a little late this morning." The students laughed in surprise: they had expected her to react as an enemy, but she had just joined their side. She had

154

loosened up enough to be clever and funny, something kids admire, and so the conflict was over.

I used a similar technique twenty years ago when I was starting a job as a group home houseparent for eight teenage boys. In my first week on the job I had not yet earned a place in the group, and so when I disciplined Paul, he felt resentment. The fact that he was small for his age and I'm six-foot-four didn't help. Anyway, that night as I was drifting off to sleep, I heard two muffled voices in the next room. As I listened more voices were added; soon I counted at least five. Then Paul's voice, sounding as baritone as he could make it, said, "Let's tie them up with wire in the attic until they meet our demands." After ten minutes I heard no more. But the next morning at breakfast, I had to face the problem: because of me, the boys had now talked themselves into a campaign against all four houseparents. I could have been confrontational and threatening, but that would have aggravated the problem. I could have been businesslike and scheduled a "family meeting." Instead I tried an indirect approach. Between spoonfuls of cereal I casually said, "Guys, I'm going to the hardware store this morning—could I pick up anything? They're having a big sale on wire!" At first they tensed up, but as they saw me smile, they laughed. We all relaxed, and then I explained that I was brand-new to this place and didn't know how things worked. I asked them to be patient and to let me know when something I did bothered them. They opened up and told me how hard it was adjusting to new houseparents. We laughed a lot through the discussion, and ended up feeling like a family.

Obviously, my humorous approach to defusing this conflict wasn't the only way to handle it, but it worked far better than other methods I saw. Another houseparent, a part-time karate instructor as tall as I am but twice as big across the shoulders, had no sense of humor, and met every problem head-on. When we agreed at a staff meeting that one boy's gerbil village had gotten too populous (twenty-eight), this houseparent went up to the boy's room to announce the verdict. His direct confrontational style angered the boy, and when he left the room, the boy followed him to the top of the stairs, where he kicked him in the middle of the back. The man fell down the stairs, breaking his arm, and the next day he handed in his resignation. That was a powerful lesson for everyone in the house about how not to handle disagreements. As an exercise at this point, you might try to think up a humorous way to persuade a fourteen-year-old boy to get rid of two dozen gerbils.

Humor can even save lives. In the 1850s, before becoming President, Abraham Lincoln was challenged to a duel. He accepted the challenge, provided that he could choose the weapons and the distance. The other gentleman agreed. "Cow shit at five paces," said Lincoln. And the conflict was over. Had Lincoln not had his marvelous sense of humor, he might well have been killed in the duel, and would never have become President Lincoln.

Several police departments have been trained in the use of humor to handle family fights. In Troy, New York, police officers worked out a routine for responding to family fights in which one officer arrived in uniform and the other arrived dressed as Bugs Bunny. The sheer incongruity here derailed the combatants' train of thought and emotion, clearing their minds for a moment. They stepped out of their confrontational mode. In laughing, most of them calmed down and were able to talk out their problems.

In California, police officer Adelle Roberts showed remarkable quick-wittedness in responding to a family fight.[12] As she pulled up to the house, there was yelling and screaming; as she approached the front door a television set came crashing through a second-story window. To be heard over the din, she knocked loudly. "Who is it?" bellowed an angry voice. "TV repair!" she answered. Amused and a littled confused, the couple stopped fighting and came to the door. Their problems still had to be worked out, but now they were past their anger and able to discuss things. If Roberts' opening line had been the standard "Police! Come out with your hands up!" they might well have kept fighting, or turned their violence against her.

The next time trouble is brewing, and it looks as though a heated argument is imminent, try a little nonthreatening humor to clear people's heads for a moment, and get them to relax with each other.

The Possibilities Are Unlimited

We've been looking at situations in which humor can make people feel less defensive and so be more clearheaded and cooperative. We've considered persuasion, training, educating, announcing bad news, apologizing, handling unreasonable complaints, commanding, warning, evaluating, criticizing, and handling conflict. But we could continue the list with complaining, saying no, accepting praise, and lots of others. In any social situation where it helps to get people to relax, a little humor can have a big effect.

157

HANDLE IT WITH HUMOR—GROUP EXERCISES

Exercise 6-2

1. Your work load is as heavy as you lcan take. In fact, you've been thinking of asking for an assistant. But your boss walks in and asks if you could do one more job by tomorrow.

Discuss what might happen if you:

A. Get angry.

B. Meekly say, "I'll try my best."

C. Use humorous exaggeration to let your boss know that you can't take on any more work. For example: "Right now, I don't even have time to _____?

2. Have each member of the group describe a recent interpersonal problem at work. After each description, brainstorm to come up with three humorous ways to handle the problem. Then discuss the pros and cons of the three suggestions.

Notes

1   *Newsweek*, August 26, 1963, pp. 74-75.

2   These studies are cited by Steve Wilson in *The Art of Mixing Work and Play* (Columbus, OH: Applied Humor Systems, 1992), pp. 116-117.

3   Don Oldenburg, "The Bottom Line is Laughter," *Washington Post*, March 4, 1986, B5.

4   Bob Basso and Judi Klosek, *This Job Should Be Fun* (Holbrook MA: Bob Adams, 1991), p. 25.

5   Dorothy Markiewicz, "Can Humor Increase Persuasion Or Is It All a Joke?" Paper presented at Speech Communication Association, Chicago, December 1972.

6   Lynette McCullough, "The Potential for Using Humor in Global Advertising," 1993. Unpublished paper.

7   Regina Barreca, *They Used to Call Me Snow White . . . But I Drifted: Women's Strategic Use of Humor* (New York: Viking, 1991), p. 142.

8   Malcolm Kushner, *Lighten Up: How to Use Humor for Business Success* (New York: Simon and Schuster, 1990), pp. 118-119.

9   Steve Wilson, *The Art of Mixing Work and Play* (Columbus, OH: Applied Humor Systems, 1992), pp. 82-83.

10   "Corporate Comedy," *Industry Week*, February 17, 1986, p. 22.

11   Steve Wilson, *The Art of Mixing Work and Play* (Columbus, OH: Applied Humor Systems, 1992), p. 39.

12   Malcolm Kushner, *Lighten Up: How to Use Humor for Business Success* (New York: Simon and Schuster, 1990), p. 108.

CHAPTER 7

HUMOR IN FORMAL COMMUNICATIONS

The Benefits of Humor in Communication

We have already seen a lot about how humor enhances informal communication. In this chapter we'll look at humor in speeches, presentations, correspondence, and other kinds of formal communication. When experts rank the most important skills of executives, the ability to communicate is usually at the top of the list. And no wonder. According to a study published in *Business Week*, there are 33 million presentations, sales meetings, and training classes going on in American corporations every day.[1]

Top-level executives spend 94 percent of their day in communication activities, middle managers spend about 80 percent, and first level managers about 70 percent.[2] And among communication skills, the ability to use humor is one of the most versatile and important.

One value of humor in communication we have already seen—its ability to get and hold people's attention. Everyone is bombarded with hundreds of spoken and written messages a day, and humor helps a message stand out from the clutter. Because humor often depends on small details, too, people pay *close* attention to a message in which they are looking for humor.

They also *remember* a funny message up to 800 percent better, according to some studies. We remember something to the extent that it has impact on us. If I ask you to recall one experience from your childhood, it probably won't be brushing your teeth or taking your socks off, although you did these things thousands of times. What you'll probably remember is some experience that made you laugh or cry.

When I lived in northern California, I did a lot of driving. I have forgotten the repetitive commuting. But I do remember driving just once past a sign near Sonoma that said:

PRECISION ENGINEERING COMPANY
103 YARDS, 2 FEET, 9 INCHES AHEAD.

If I moved to Sonoma and found myself in need of engineering services, I'm sure I'd think of Precision Engineering right away.

Humor has such impact that it can even make us "remember" what didn't happen. Most people who know about the Stock Market Crash of 1929 will tell you that because of the crash, hundreds of ruined investors jumped out of tall buildings. But that isn't true. What people are remembering is all the newspaper *cartoons* from 1929 that showed investors jumping from buildings.

Advertisers, of course, are in the business of getting people to remember messages, and that's why they use humor so much. As a little test, can you finish this phrase from a TV commercial?

"I can't believe I . . ."?

Did you say "ate the whole thing"? Do you realize that Alka-Seltzer commercial was on TV over twenty-five years ago? From a more recent commercial, can you finish this line?

"Where's the ____?"

Did you picture the woman saying "Where's the beef?" in the Wendy's commercial?

Not only does humor get your message noticed and remembered, but it creates rapport, getting your audience to relax, identify with you, and be receptive to your message.

Humor is especially useful when you are trying to warm people to something they consider to be over their heads or beyond their interest. When IBM unveiled its personal computer, for instance, it wanted people to stop thinking of IBM's intimidating mainframe computers, and start thinking of a machine for their homes that was as user-friendly as a portable typewriter. So it was perfectly natural that IBM used a Charlie Chaplin look-alike for its ads.

In situations where someone might feel uncomfortable or embarrassed, humor can also be helpful. When I was in college, I noticed that among the lines men used to meet women, the funny ones were considerably more successful. In bars my friend Gary used to bend over slightly and look at the floor near the woman's feet. When she looked at him, he'd say "Excuse me, did you happen to see my Congressional Medal of Honor around here?"

Even when something threatening happens, a humorous message can rescue us. Consider this letter to *Working Woman* magazine[3]:

> I read with interest your story on humor at work . . . and it reminded me of a recent business trip that could have been a disaster if my boss's sense of humor hadn't saved the situation.
>
> We had to make an elaborate slide presentation to a major client in San Francisco. When we got there we found that our equipment wasn't working. There we were, with a room full of executive vice presidents, a case full of slides and no projector.
>
> The rest of us started to panic, but my boss didn't miss a beat. She made a quip about how nothing beats a live performance and then had our six-person sales team line up according to size to form a bar graph showing market growth! Our audience appreciated our sense of humor, and what's more, we got the account.

Three Guidelines

Now although humor has tremendous potential in communications, many people use it poorly. In fact, some people's attempts at humor backfire more often than they work. Seeing them bomb, many of their colleagues shy away from even trying humor. Maybe you are one of them. If so, let me suggest some guidelines for making your humor work. I'll concentrate on speeches and presentations, adding a few comments at the end about humor in letters and memos.

In using humor in a speech or presentation, there are three general guidelines. First, be sensitive to your audience. Second, make your speech conversational. And third, maximize surprise. We'll look at these one at a time.

Be Sensitive to Your Audience

In preparing a speech, you should pay attention to the characteristics of who's listening—age and gender, for example—and to subtler issues such as their current concerns. Humor that went over well with your close friends might bomb with a large audience of strangers. The story that your colleagues enjoyed so much might be offensive to your clients. And there are some occasions where no humor might be appropriate.

The most basic step you need to take in a speech is to create rapport with your audience. Here are some ways to do it.

1. Use the kind of language to which the audience is accustomed. Different groups have their own ways of saying things, and their own taboos about what can be said at all. When I speak to older people, my vocabulary and pool of examples are more restricted than when I talk to college students. I often tell the story (in Chapter 6) about the time Abraham Lincoln was challenged to a duel. The last line ("Cow shit at five paces") might be acceptable to college students, but not for a banquet of retired folks, who would rather hear "Cow manure at five paces."

2. Don't use humor that accentuates your power or status. That will turn people with lower status against you. For example, in a presentation to her division regarding an upcoming reorganization of staff, a high-level manager tried to ease tensions with a wisecrack about a colleague who "will soon be moving out of his plush office into a cubicle." She thought of this as good-natured kidding, but she had not considered that most of the people in her audience spent every working day in cubicles. They felt alienated by her comment. When Henry Ford had a disagreement with his managers, he would sometimes take them outside the building and point to the word "FORD" above the door. "Now whose name is that?" he would ask. That was hardly funny; it was just intimidation. The managers usually buckled under and did what Ford wanted, of course, but as they did they were full of resentment.

3. Make sure your humor doesn't make you seem insensitive to your audience's feelings. Don't make light of some big problem its members face. In discussing an impending layoff, for example, there is probably no way to use humor.

4. For the same reason, in important matters never use humor as an evasive tactic as a way of not responding to someone's legitimate concerns. If you are in charge and are asked about the possibility of a layoff, for example, you shouldn't make a wisecrack to avoid the question. Either answer the question honestly, or if you're not free to talk about it, say so.

5. Don't ridicule individuals or groups, either people in your audience or people outside. If those being ridiculed are present, you will alienate them, probably forever. And even if your targets are not part of your group, some members of your audience will sympathize with them, and will turn against you. Remember that your humor is supposed to reduce friction, espe-

cially feelings of threat. If your humor is hostile—to anyone—at least part of your audience will feel threatened.

6. In advising against ridicule here, I am not saying that you should never poke fun at people. But when you do, do it in a positive way that accepts them as it focuses on their foibles. Good-natured kidding or joshing has none of the hostility of ridicule; it allows people to acknowledge their mistakes and problems, and still feel secure in the group. Indeed, kidding is an important part of being accepted in the group. We don't kid enemies or strangers, but only those to whom we feel close. There is even the institution of the "roast"—the banquet at which a person's friends give speeches full of wisecracks about the guest of honor. That's a mark of honor and affection.

But remember that for kidding to work, closeness is required. In writing a speech, you may think of a great wisecrack about someone in the organization, but unless you know that person well, you shouldn't even consider using it. Only our friends have our permission to kid us. Anyone else will probably be resented if he or she tries.

Even closeness to people is not enough for you to kid them in a speech: your audience must *realize* that you are close. At a big business meeting where few in the audience knew the main speaker, a friend of his did the introduction. Then the speaker came to the microphone and started with this quip: "Thank you, Frank. You know, Frank is the opposite of E.F. Hutton. When Frank talks, nobody listens." Now at a luncheon given for Frank by his friends, that crack might have been funny, but in a large group of people who didn't know Frank or the person he had introduced, it came across as unmotivated hostility, making everyone uncomfortable.[4]

Make It Conversational

The most believable and influential presentations usually sound like good conversation. That's because the closest rapport possible in communication is between two individuals. So even if you are talking to a thousand people, make it sound like you are talking to each of them as an individual. Here are some ways to do that.

1. As the person introducing you finishes the introduction, move energetically up to the podium, and with a smile look around at the people you'll be talking to.

2. If it's appropriate, show concern for their comfort by asking questions such as, "Is it too chilly in here for you?" or "Can those in the back see this diagram?" This is the kind of friendly gesture a good host would make, and you'll get instant rapport. Make sure in advance, of course, that you can meet their requests, should they have any.

3. In your opening remarks, thank the individuals who brought you there, mentioning them by name, and gesturing toward them. They will appreciate the attention, and the rest of the audience will see you as a gracious person. Say something, too, about the group and the occasion. That brings you and your audience together, and makes its members feel good about themselves.

4. As you talk, move around and use gestures. Nothing is harder to listen to than a talking head peeking over a lectern. If you wear glasses, take them off occasionally. If there's a microphone on a cord, take it out of the stand and walk around. If you want more freedom of movement, ask (well in advance) for a wireless hand-held or lavaliere microphone.

5. One feature of conversations that makes them such an effective form of communication is the eye contact

involved. We naturally expect people who are talking to us to look at us. So as you begin your talk, look for an individual to engage with your eyes. Once your eyes meet, look for signs that he or she is agreeing with you. Then smile, and move your gaze to someone in the other side of the audience. When he or she acknowledges you, move your gaze to a third person, and so on for the rest of your presentation.

6. Get your audience to participate in your presentation in non-threatening ways. Its members will automatically be more interested, and will remember the presentation better. As in life generally, we remember those occasions in which we are actively involved.

One way to seek involvement is to ask your audience to remember or imagine certain scenarios: "Think of your favorite beach." "Remember the kid in grade school who was always late?" "What would chairs look like if our knees bent the other way?"

With small groups, you can get more involvement by having individuals do something like stand up and answer questions. You might even have an exercise they could all do with each other. With large groups it's safest to have the entire audience do something together.

7. Good speeches, like good conversations, have spontaneity. Much of it comes from variations in volume, pitch, and speed—good speeches are not read in a monotone.

Of course a speech requires preparation. But preparing a good speech is not practicing a script; it's getting a group of ideas organized so well in your head that you can talk about them effortlessly. For that you should work not from a text but from an outline or a set of note cards.

I outline my talks on 2 1/4-inch by 4-inch Rolodex® cards, and arrange them in a horizontal card holder with section dividers. The cards are color coded to help me check everything before the presentation. If a card has me show a transparency or slide, I put that card in a blue plastic sleeve. A card in a red sleeve means that I will hold up a prop. An orange sleeve means that the audience will be asked to participate. The card holder goes on the lectern, and I flip through the cards as I give the talk. I can't lose my place as I could using large pieces of paper, and 99 percent of the time my eyes are on the people I'm talking to.

While spontaneity is important in all speeches, it is especially important in humor. Other things being equal, spontaneous humor will seem funnier. Speakers who save themselves from an embarrassing moment on stage with a clever quip, often get bigger laughs from that spontaneous comment than from any of their prepared humor.

In the 1992 presidential debates on TV, each candidate's speaking time was tightly regulated. In answering a question, Ross Perot was saying that the next president would have to fix the problems left by Presidents Reagan and Bush. He was in the middle of a sentence—"The party's over; it's time for the clean-up crew . . ."—when the moderator broke in, "Time is up." Without missing a beat Perot quipped, "Yes, it is." By making that stage direction sound like the last line of his answer, Perot not only saved himself the embarrassment of ending mid-sentence, but scored points for his spontaneous wit.

One thing that spontaneous humor conveys is the speaker's control of the situation. Consider the woman who was in the middle of her banquet speech when a busboy began clearing the dishes from a table in front of the podium. He intended no harm, but everyone's attention was drawn away from her. She stopped speaking, smiled, and gestured toward the busboy, "Of course, you all know my husband." All eyes came back to her; the young man got the hint and stopped clearing the table. She had reestablished control.

Now she may have used that line before; she may have even borrowed it from another speaker. But it came across as spontaneous, and so was effective. Similarly, in the 1992 TV debates, when Ross Perot was asked about the feasibility of his proposed gasoline tax, his self-effacing answer—"If you've got another plan, I'm all ears"—sounded spontaneous and so worked, even though he had used it before. The obvious lesson here is that even if you have made some quip or told some funny story a hundred times, you should make it *sound* like you are creating it on the spot.

8. The humor in a speech should also be integrated into the message, as humor is in a conversation. It should not be a bribe added to the speech to keep the audience paying attention.

It is especially important that the humor not interrupt and distract from the flow of ideas. Instead it should be part of that flow.

Unfortunately, there is a venerable tradition in public speaking in which a talk is prepared, and then one or more unrelated or barely related jokes are added to it, often from a joke book that's twenty years out of date. But even a very funny joke stuck onto the beginning of a boring talk won't save the talk. If the joke is funny, a few people may listen for another joke, but they won't listen carefully to the talk itself. When the presentation is over, at best they will remember the jokes.

So choose your humor carefully, making sure that it is connected to your topic and that it reinforces your message.

9. In addition to sharing your ideas with your audience, share something of yourself. That creates rapport. In listening to a speech, just as in conversation, we are naturally more interested in hearing something that's part of the speaker's life—his or her experiences, concerns, or point of view—than we are in hearing impersonal facts or stories. That's why successful comedians personalize their material whenever possible. They don't tell stories that begin, "A guy walked into a laundromat but had forgotten to bring change." They say, "Last week I walked into a laundromat but had forgotten my roll of quarters."

So personalize your humor. For stories, draw from your own experience, or borrow from other people's experience, changing the details to make it sound like it happened to you.

All of us have funny things happening to us every day, and when we get together with friends, some of our best fun is trading funny experiences. Unfortunately, we tend to forget these stories quickly. If you want to have a good collection of stories to use in presentations, make it a habit to write down the best ones soon after the event, and save them in a file.

10. In personalizing your presentations, one of the best techniques is self-effacing humor, poking fun at some odd feature or shortcoming of your own. This is especially useful in creating rapport at the beginning of a talk. In his book *Lighten Up,* Malcolm Kushner offers the example of Fred Hoar, a Silicon Valley advertising executive, who begins his speeches by making fun of the unfortunate sound of his name: "My name is Fred Hoar. That's spelled F-R-E-D."[5] Kushner himself uses a

more biting piece of self-effacing humor as his introduction. "Eight years ago I practiced law with an international corporate law firm in San Francisco. Today I'm
a humor consultant. Now, whether or not you think
the world needs a humor consultant, I'm sure you'll
agree we can use one less attorney."[6] Self-effacing
humor is also useful for deflecting criticism. As we've
said before, if you are pointing out your own shortcomings, other people aren't likely to attack you. The
great advantage you have in a speech is that the shortcomings you poke fun at can be small or innocent
ones, instead of the big ones your opponents would
have brought up. In the Lincoln-Douglas debates in the
1850s, for example, Douglas accused Lincoln of holding incompatible policies. He called him "two-faced." In
his rebuttal, Lincoln answered, "Ladies and gentlemen
of the audience, I leave it to you: if I had two faces,
would I be wearing this one?" Everyone laughed and
Lincoln quickly changed the topic. By joking about his
homeliness he had short-circuited Douglas' criticism of
something more serious.

In creating self-effacing humor, look for things for
which you aren't responsible—like your name or your
looks—or small mistakes and faults. Don't engage in
heavy confessions or self-ridicule. You want to show
people that you're humble, not that you deserve to be
indicted. Just as when you are kidding other people, in
kidding yourself you should show that you accept
yourself as a valuable human being.

The humility expressed by self-effacing humor can
even be the humility of the group instead of just the
speaker's humility. In fact, expressing the group's
humility can bring its members closer to the speaker
and to each other. At a White House dinner honoring
Nobel Prize winners, for example, President John
Kennedy said, "I think this is the most extraordinary

collection of talent, of human knowledge, that has ever been gathered together at the White House— with the possible exception of when Thomas Jefferson dined alone."

Self-effacing humor is also useful when others are praising rather than criticizing you. Indeed, it's the standard way to accept a compliment graciously. It shows that you see yourself objectively and do not have an inflated sense of your importance. When John Kennedy was asked by a young boy, "Mr. President, how did you become a war hero?" he answered, "It was absolutely involuntary. They sank my boat."

11. Personalize your humor in the other direction, as well: tailor it to your audience. As mentioned earlier, you should make some comments at the beginning about the occasion and the group, as a friendly conversational gesture. And in your presentation, talk about situations with which your audience is familiar. If possible, work in comments and stories about people present; that will automatically interest them and others in the audience. If the audience consists of your colleagues, you already know what they are interested in. If it's made up of strangers, do a little research.

More generally, anchor your humor, and your entire talk, in the concrete world of familiarity. Give your talk impact the way comedians do: use lots of realistic details, especially visually striking descriptions. In general, the more specific and graphic your descriptions are, the more vivid your audience's mental pictures will be, and the greater the impact of your message.

Woody Allen's humor is full of examples of the power of specificity. In his movie *Annie Hall*, Allen's character gets a phone call from his girlfriend asking him to come over to get rid of a big spider in her bathroom. He walks into the bathroom confidently, but comes out wide-eyed and shaken. "You've got a spider in there *the size of a Buick*," he says. Notice how much less funny this line would be if he said "car," a general term, instead of "Buick," a specific term.

So in your stories, don't say "I walked into a restaurant," but "I walked into Denny's," or better "Last Tuesday night I walked into _____(the name of a local restaurant your audience knows well)."

12. Let me finish these tips on making humor conversational by discouraging you from using two common kinds of humor—jokes and puns.

It may sound strange to have a humor expert warning you against telling jokes, especially when many people *equate* humor with jokes, but consider how jokes violate almost all the advice I've given so far about making your humor conversational. A joke isn't spontaneous—it's a script that the joke-teller recites. The teller didn't even create the joke; in fact, no one knows where it came from! It's not based on the teller's experiences; it's not even a true story. And while telling a personal anecdote is a completely natural move in a conversation, telling a joke interrupts the conversation.

Good evidence of the big difference between stories and jokes is the fact that although almost everyone can get a laugh with a funny story, few people have much success with jokes. In surveys, typically only 5 percent of respondents rate themselves as good at joke-telling, while 89 percent of respondents in one study rated themselves as "above average" in their sense of humor!

If you do tell jokes, keep them short. The longer your audience has to listen to the set-up of the joke, the higher their expectations will be, and the funnier your punchline has to be. A ten-second joke that bombs is quickly forgotten. But if your joke is three minutes long and doesn't get a laugh, your audience has wasted three minutes and there's only you to blame. In fact, it is likely to remember your presentation largely as the talk containing that awful joke that went on forever.

The other kind of humor to be avoided is puns. Puns have two advantages over jokes: they are usually spontaneous, and they are usually created by the person saying them. Unfortunately, however, most puns are based simply on coincidences of how certain words sound, not on anything deeper, like our common experiences. And by calling attention to words themselves, they interrupt the flow of the conversation. At their best, which isn't often, puns display mere cleverness. It's this cleverness more than anything else that makes their creators laugh in *self-congratulation*. The listeners don't feel this triumph, however, and so they usually smile politely, or moan softly.

Maximize Surprise

Our first two guidelines, about being sensitive to your audience and making your talk conversational, apply not just to humor but to speeches generally. Our third guideline, to maximize surprise, pertains especially to humor.

Humor, as we have seen, is enjoying incongruity. It is getting a pleasurable jolt from having our mental patterns violated. To create humor for an audience, then, you should catch its members offguard, hit them with something they aren't ready for.

Unfortunately, many speakers who attempt humor don't pay attention to the importance of surprise. They think of a funny story or joke, and then they try to convey the pleasant feeling they had when they heard the punchline. Instead of *telling* the story or joke, so that their listeners will go through the same mental gymnastics they went through as they heard it, they *summarize* it or simply *describe* it. But a summary or a description of a funny story can't have the effect that telling the story has. To make the audience laugh, you need to carefully take it through the set-up, and then surprise it with the punchline.

In general, the more surprise you achieve in your humor, the more effective it is. Here are some tips for achieving surprise.

1. Never announce that you are going to be funny. Don't start a story or joke with "Did you hear the one about...?" or "Here's a funny story." That reduces the surprise.

2. For the same reason, don't give a summary or description of the story you're going to tell; just tell it.

3. Avoid phrases such as "You'll die laughing at this one!" That's presumptuous. When you tell people that they'll find your story sidesplittingly funny, you're implicitly saying that you know their taste inside and out, and can predict their responses. That's at least mildly insulting, like telling them that they will love the wine you're about to serve. People like to be amused, but what each of us finds amusing is personal: it depends on our experiences, our intelligence, and our taste. Don't pre-empt your audience's judgment. If you want to please people with your favorite wine, just serve it—they'll decide if they like it or not. If you want to tell them a funny story, just tell it and let them decide if it's hilarious.

When someone tells me that the story he or she is about to tell is hysterical, I want to shout, "I'll be the judge of that!" And I know others who react that way too. We feel as if we've been challenged. As Malcolm Kushner says, we put a "comedy chip" on our shoulders.[7] You avoid all these problems when you don't announce that your story is funny.

4. For these same reasons—*not* to reduce the audience's surprise and *not* to second-guess it—don't laugh at your own humor, especially not during the telling. That signals your listeners to expect the punchline, and it sends the arrogant message that because you're laughing, they'll have to laugh too. Take a cue from stand-up comics, who don't laugh at their own humor. The last well-known comedian I can remember who did was Red Skelton, and his comedy suffered accordingly.

5. To create the mental jolts of humor, keep everything short. In effective messages generally, each word counts. The Declaration of Independence set up a whole new system of government in just 1,400 words. In humor, economy is especially important: brevity, as Shakespeare said, is the soul of wit. The best humor sets up the audience's expectations quickly, and then suddenly violates them. And as noted above, the longer people listen to the set-up of the story, the greater is their investment in the story, and the greater the jolt at the end must be to repay their attention. A long, complicated story or joke will lose many in the audience, but worse, it raises the expectations of those who follow it to the end.

Mastery and Failure

If you follow these guidelines, you're well on your way to using humor effectively in your presentations. But let me offer a few final tips.

The first is that creating humor involves skills that few speakers master. If these skills were easy, there'd be a lot more rich stand-up comedians, and many fewer after-dinner speakers talking for free.

In order to achieve the mental jolt you want in your audience, you have to choose your words carefully, make every word and gesture count, and get everything in the right order. And you have to make it all seem like effortless conversation—if you look like you're trying hard to be funny, your audience will tighten up and won't laugh.

To become skilled at humor in presentations, take advantage of every opportunity to give presentations, and put at least some humor in every one.

When practicing your presentation, stand in front of a mirror and talk into a tape recorder. Play it back several times to see where you can improve. If you can use a camcorder, that's even better, because it will highlight your actual physical characteristics as they would appear to others. For years I listened to audiotapes of my various presentations, but until I saw myself on TV, I didn't realize that I had two nervous habits—putting my index finger to the side of my nose, and tightening my neck muscles. Those habits stopped instantly once I saw them. If you are stiff or make odd gestures, you may not be aware of these until you view yourself on tape.

Practice your stories with friends in conversation, too. Don't announce that you're practicing. Just work the story into an appropriate part of the conversation, and see if it gets a good response. If it does, that's a good sign it can work in a speech.

Last, some tips about failure. Even if you've mastered your material and presentation, you're not going to bat a thousand. No one does. After your best quip or funniest story, there will be at least one person in the audience who will not laugh or maybe even smile. And sometimes that number will be much higher. How should you respond? Keep going, just as you would in a conversation.

If you're lucky, your humor went over their heads; they didn't realize that you were trying to make them laugh. In my talks, for example, I often mention that for years humor researchers held their national convention on April 1. Usually, people make the connection with April Fools' Day and smile or laugh. But occasionally no one makes the connection. Then I simply keep going, and no one's the wiser.

When your humor goes over your listeners' heads, the last thing you want to do is repeat or call attention to what they missed—that has no chance of making them laugh, and worse, it makes them look stupid. It emphasizes the difference between you and them, killing whatever rapport you have established.

For similar reasons, don't ever apologize for a failed joke or story. That just highlights your failure and keeps it at the center of their attention. Unless your listeners are hostile, they don't want to dwell on your failure; they just want you to move on to something that will interest them.

Here we can see another way in which anecdotes are preferable to fictional jokes, and relevant humor to irrelevant humor. If you're telling a joke unrelated to your topic and it bombs, you have failed *completely*: you tried to make your audience laugh but it didn't. If, on the other hand, to illustrate a point you use a true story that you consider funny, and your audience doesn't laugh, then you have still made your point. In fact, unless you promised people that the story would be funny, they might not even realize that you've failed to amuse them. A relevant story that doesn't make your audience laugh still keeps your presentation moving along, while a joke that bombs interrupts the flow of your presentation.

What if a story or joke *really* bombs? What if everyone understands that you were trying to be funny but you failed? Then consider going to Plan B—make fun of the failure of the humor.

I call this "metahumor;" the incongruity is that what was supposed to be funny, wasn't. The master of metahumor was Johnny Carson, who for decades had "savers" prepared for those occasions his jokes bombed. He would glance at his watch and yawn. He would pretend to crumple up a piece of paper (on which the joke was supposedly written) and toss it. He would signal the band to begin a vaudeville tune, and would start dancing as a distractionary tactic. Or like a lion tamer, he would pick up an imaginary chair and hold it between him and the supposedly hostile audience.

Metahumor is useful in several ways. It acknowledges what everyone is painfully aware of—that the humor failed—and so it clears the air. It also prevents the audience from turning against you. In admitting that your humor bombed, you have come over to its side. And if your metahumor is reasonably clever, it will get the laugh you were looking for. Johnny Carson was often funniest precisely when making fun of how bad that night's jokes were. You may even want to prepare Carson–like come-back lines for when your humor doesn't go over.

The above is a worst case scenario, where no one laughs at your humor. Normally, some people will laugh and some won't. As long as a good number, say half, are laughing, don't worry; just keep going. You'll never reach everyone through humor. If some people have faces of stone even in what you consider the funniest parts of your talk, don't assume that they're dissatisfied with you. It may be just the mood they're in. Or they may be humor-impaired from a lifetime of suppressing playfulness. They didn't laugh, but they didn't expect to, so you haven't failed them. As long as your comic material is relevant and moves the presentation along, they'll be satisfied.

Humor in Written Communications

We've been discussing humor in oral presentations, but it also works in letters and memos. Written communications in the workplace have traditionally been even more formal, impersonal, and boring than speeches, and humor can help on all these scores. It can make a letter or memo interesting—even fun—to read, much like a letter from a friend.

Fortunately in recent years, business writing has become more conversational, especially with the growth of fax and electronic mail, which because of their speed and convenience are inherently less formal than paper mail. There may be a few holdouts who still write "Please be advised that we are in receipt of your letter," but most of us now write "Thank you for your letter." It requires less writing or dictating, less typing, and less reading.

And it's more like the spoken word—we certainly would never *say* "Please be advised that we are in receipt of" instead of "Thank you for."

Putting humor into memos, letters, faxes and e-mail is an important part of this trend toward informality and friendliness. And it's showing up in more and more business correspondence. Recently, when I let my subscription to a computer magazine lapse, for example, I received this letter:

Dear Subscriber:

No doubt, our last invoice is sitting right there on your desk, buried under a stack of papers. I understand.

That's why I'm sending you this friendly reminder to let you know your subscription payment is now due.

Won't you please retrieve our invoice from underneath your stack of papers—or use the one enclosed—and return it with your check now? That way you'll have one less paper to worry about.

The letter is signed "Jerry _____, Editor-in-Chief." Next to the first paragraph, in what looks like blue handwriting, is the note "I have the same stack on my desk," and next to the last paragraph is another note, "I'd appreciate it."

Although this is a form letter mailed out by the thousands, and its purpose is to get people to pay up, it is designed to look like a personal letter from someone who cares. Its gentle humor reduces readers' defensiveness toward its potentially threatening message, and persuades them to send in their checks.

A more striking example of the growing informality of business communications is a clever book entitled *FAX THIS BOOK!*[8] It consists of over one hundred tear-out cover sheets for fax transmissions—for memos, dunning letters, purchase orders, shipping instructions, publicity releases, proofs of delivery, etc. Like a funny greeting card, each cover sheet combines a cartoon drawing with an attention-grabbing heading. On the graphic for a fax requesting a meeting, for instance, a person is only partly drawn in—the rest is dots with small numbers next to them. The text reads "Would you pencil me in? I'd like to meet with you!" Another cover sheet has a business person at a desk with a cloud of black smoke hovering overhead: "Remember that idea we put on the back burner? I think we need to discuss it!"

Perhaps the most serious piece of business correspondence is the debt-collection letter, but here too humor can work. One technique is to make the debtor sympathetic to the plight of the debtee through funny exaggeration. An advertising agency in Virginia uses four cartoons to handle overdue accounts.[9] The first, sent at thirty days, depicts a dog asking for payment. The second, at sixty days, shows the dog depressed. At ninety days, the debtee is crushed under a pile of bills, and at 120 days there's a tearful man kneeling in a pool of blood with a knife in his back. According to the president of the company, payment of overdue bills has increased 17 percent since he started using these cartoons.

At a seminar I did for a group of credit managers, a woman showed me a rubber stamp she uses for overdue accounts. Having it made cost her $14.95—she estimates that it has saved her hundreds of hours in correspondence, and the company thousands of dollars.

> Hello there, I'm the Company Computer. So far, only I know that you haven't been making regular payments on your account. However, if I don't process a payment from you within 10 days, I will have to tell a human.

Or how about this closing paragraph from a collection letter?

> We appreciate your business, but please give us a break. Your account is overdue ten months. This means we've carried you longer than your mother did.

The examples used so far are of communications with strangers. When you're writing to colleagues or clients you know well, you can use humor that is more familiar and humor that is more outlandish.

For people I know well, I make my own "Truth Is Stranger than Fiction" stationery from a file of odd clippings from newpapers, magazines, and catalogs. There's a pet shop ad, "Ferrets 20 percent Off"; a line from a magazine ad, "Is Your Bladder Controlling Your Life?"; and a headline from a weekly tabloid, "WOMAN DIVORCES SIAMESE TWIN TO WED HIS BROTHER." I also clip selections from the "Harper's Index" in *Harper's* magazine each month, which is a list of statistics like the following:

- Price of having one's hair set in dreadlocks at Slug Hair Salon in Tokyo: $1,215.

- Percentage of incarcerated burglars who say they looked at their victims' family photo albums: 32.

- Price of a lunch of lobster, asparagus, and poached pears, at the Treasury Department executive dining room: $4.75.

I stick one of these items to the top of a plain piece of paper, put the paper on the photocopying machine, and out comes my stationery. Amid my colleagues' stacks of otherwise boring and forgettable mail, it provides a moment of delight and gets them to remember me.

A "Truth Is Stranger than Fiction" file, by the way, is also useful in writing articles and speeches, and for spicing up conversations. All it takes to collect are a pair of scissors and a file folder. Many newspapers feature at least one bizarre story each day—usually among the national news items. Four national tabloids are filled with such stories: the *National Enquirer*, the *National Examiner*, the *Star*, and *Weekly World News*.

Happy clipping!

Notes

1   Ron Hoff, *"I Can See You Naked" : A Fearless Guide to Making Great Presentations* (Kansas City: Andrews and McMeel, 1988), p. 30.

2   Bob Ross, *Laugh, Lead, and Profit* (San Diego: Arrowhead, 1989), p. 73.

3   *Working Woman*, June 1991, p. 20.

4   Gregory Salsbury, "Ice-Breaker or Ice-Maker," *Management World,* January 1986, p. 31.

5   Malcolm Kushner, *Lighten Up: How to Use Humor for Business Success* (New York: Simon and Schuster, 1990), pp. 77-78.

6   Ibid., p.77.

7   Ibid., p. 30.

8   John Caldwell, *FAX THIS BOOK!* (New York: Workman, 1990).

9   Malcolm Kushner, *Lighten Up: How to Use Humor for Business Success* (New York: Simon and Schuster, 1990), p. 122.

CHAPTER 8

MIRTHFUL MANAGEMENT

When the Going Gets Tough, the Smart Lighten Up

I n the last decade and a half, the American work place has gone through huge changes. Increased foreign and domestic competition has driven many companies out of business, and several of our most respected corporations have reported huge losses. Big companies have been restructured and downsized. During the 1980s the Fortune 500 companies lost three million jobs. Between 1985 and 1995, the nation's largest companies eliminated one quarter of their workforces.

In this volatile and stressful climate, many people think that they should hunker down, take as few risks as possible, and eliminate every hint of playfulness from their work. Like the Third Little Pig living in Big Bad Wolf country, they put their noses to the grindstone and shoulders to the wheel, and hope that by their workaholism they'll survive the next layoff.

But if you look at the people who are making it in today's volatile business climate, their spirit is not that of the Third Little Pig. Playfulness, fun, and humor, in fact, are likely to be part of their individual work styles and their corporate culture.

Recent studies show that a sense of humor is the most consistent characteristic among executives promoted in major companies, and that managers showing a sense of humor advance faster and further than those without one.[1]

In Chapter 1 we saw an example of an executive whose sense of humor helped put him and his business on top—Herb Kelleher, CEO of Southwest Airlines. And there are whole industries known for humor and fun. One is computers. At Apple Computer the meeting rooms in one building were named after characters in *The Wizard of Oz;* in another they were named after the Seven Deadly Sins: the Greed Room, the Lust Room, etc. At Sun Microsystems, CEO Scott McNealy came to work one April 1st to find his office turned into a one-hole, par-four miniature golf course, complete with two sand traps and a birdbath. The scheme had been executed by a team of engineers, and financed by the sale of T-shirts commemorating the previous year's April Fools' Day stunt. At Versatec, another Silicon Valley firm, President Renn Zaphiropoulos works fun into the annual ceremony announcing the bonus. In 1983 he arrived on an elephant, dressed in a satin costume and accompanied by the Stanford University Marching Band. The previous spring he had announced the bonus by singing a country/western song he had composed himself.

This spirit is not limited to high-tech companies. A few years ago, Sam Walton, the billionaire founder and CEO of Wal-Mart, promised his people that he would dance a hula at dawn on Wall Street if they achieved their performance goals. When those goals were met, Walton put on a grass skirt and kept his promise. Richard

Gurin, president of Binney and Smith, makers of Crayola crayons, increased sales from $92 to $240 million betweem 1984 and 1990, largely because of his philosophy of fun. "We're focused on fun and profit," he commented, "and know that the two go together. If we are not making a lot of money, we won't be having a lot of fun. And if we're not having fun, we're probably just not making enough money."[2]

Even traditional companies like Kodak and Price-Waterhouse have installed humor rooms, as we saw in Chapter 1. In the new philosophy statement of New England Securities, the first three points are:

1. Take risks. Don't play it safe.

2. Make mistakes. Don't try to avoid them.

3. Take initiative. Don't wait for instructions.

    The last four points are:

10. Try easier, not harder.

11. Stay calm!

12. Smile!

13. Have fun!

With the massive changes occurring in American business today, humor and fun are not the only things being reevaluated. Our whole understanding of management and leadership is being revised. The traditional concept of the boss as the person who hounds people to work harder is in question, because the simple ethic of hard work is no longer working. For years Tom Peters and other experts on business trends have recommended replacing hierarchical, power-based management with the "horizontal" management of cross-functional teams.

Everyone, but especially the manager, must become more adaptable, more able to see things from different perspectives, and better at problem-solving. These and the other traits recommended by experts like Peters are precisely the features I have called mental flexibility, and humor and play foster them.

"Poke fun at the bureaucracy, bureaucrats, and the barriers that interfere with 'horizontal' management," Peters advises.[3] "Urgency and laughter go hand in hand. . . . To speed action-taking, we simply must learn to laugh at our own (personal, organizational) bureaucratic, action-delaying foibles; and we must learn to laugh at interesting and useful mistakes. In general, a spirited environment is marked by laughter—enthusiasm for being on a team and trying darn near anything to make the service or product better."[4]

This advice to change management structure and to cultivate flexibility through laughter may sound new, but astute managers knew the importance of humor all along. In his 1970 classic *Up the Organization*, Robert Townsend, former CEO of Avis, promoted much the same management style Peters talks about today, and saw its connection with humor. His checklist of the traits of a leader includes "Humorous. Has a full measure of the Comic Spirit in his make-up. Laughs even harder when the joke's on him."[5] Today we'd update the gender-biased pronouns, but the idea that leaders need humor is more valid than ever.

The Humorless Authoritarian Leader

If Townsend and Peters are right, why is it that so little attention has been paid to the values of humor in management? The answer, I think, lies in the outmoded but deep-seated authoritarian concepts of leadership which still prevail in our culture.

It's no accident that our stereotype of the boss is someone who exercises power arbitrarily, who makes many demands, who frequently criticizes but seldom praises. This style of management is not just the stuff of cartoons. Many managers rising through the ranks relish the thought of having more and more subordinates to exercise power over—or as we say, boss around.

Authoritarian leaders did not pop into existence in the 20th century. They go back thousands of years. Indeed, the pattern of a lead male dominating the group is common in primates and the higher mammals generally. In gorillas and wolves there is a hierarchy among the males—when two meet, one is dominant and the other submissive. And they test each other from time to time, changing the hierarchy as high-ranking males become old or infirm. At the head of the group is the alpha male, who dominates not only all the other males, but the females and young as well.

In human beings this system takes the form of the Emperor/General Paradigm of leadership. A powerful male dominates everyone else in the group until another male successfully challenges him and then replaces him as leader. Until the last few centuries most groups just assumed that this was the only way to organize themselves: the political or religious leader was the father figure, and the group obeyed him. Even in our supposedly democratic nation we have always tended to let the president rule like an emperor. Indeed, after throwing off the yoke of King George III in the Revolutionary War, many of the first Americans wanted to make George Washington their *king*. Washington insisted that we needed a democracy and not a King George IV, but notice that we still call him the *Father* of this country.

Under the Emperor/General Paradigm of leadership, human actions are mostly giving orders and taking orders. Leadership is wielding power, and people's importance is measured by how many have to obey them. Someone who commands a thousand people, but answers to only a few, is an important person; someone who orders nobody around is a nobody.

To maximize their power and status, leaders emphasize the differences between themselves and their subordinates. One way is by having many levels of authority in the hierarchy. Armies and big bureaucracies typically have at least a dozen. In business, status is marked by the big corner office on the top floor with the plush furniture and the private secretary, the expensive company car in the executive lot, and other "perks" that lower-level workers don't enjoy.

The leader's power over subordinates is also emphasized by the use of coercion and punishment, and by making decisions without consulting those who are affected. There's more power shown in doing something against subordinates' wishes, the perverse logic seems to go, than doing something with their approval.

Because a major source of power is knowledge, authoritarian leaders hoard knowledge. They maximize their own information while withholding it from others— even from subordinates who need it to do their jobs better. And when they make decisions, they give others a minimum of background information. That way, if the decision turns out to be foolish, they'll have a good chance of covering up the mistake; or if it is revealed, their critics won't have much to go on.

Not only mistakes are covered up, but all faults and even physical imperfections. The authoritarian leader wants agreement and obedience from everyone, and so with the help of image manipulators, pretends to be all-knowing and all-powerful. Hitler created the mythology of the invincible Führer, which his people accepted until the Allies were closing in on Berlin. A less objectionable kind of deception came out of the White House at the same time: for the twelve years Franklin Roosevelt was President, most Americans did not know that he was disabled by polio. Photographers and reporters avoided publishing any image or description of him in a wheelchair.

To maximize power, too, authoritarian leaders jealously guard their responsibilities. In corporations and other bureaucracies, a lot of time and effort goes into turf wars, each division trying to keep all its responsibilities and add more. Willingly transferring responsibilities is seen as a foolish surrender of power, no matter how much more efficient the transfer might make things.

Given their concerns with power, their inability to face their own imperfections, and their general mental rigidity, it's no surprise that authoritarian leaders have little or no sense of humor. They shun humor because it might put them on the same level as everyone else, and open them up to scrutiny. Hitler was so afraid of humor that he set up special "joke courts" for punishing people who made fun of his Nazi government. A Berlin cabaret comic who had named his horse "Adolf," for example, was sentenced to death. If authoritarian leaders laugh at all, it's likely to be scornful laughter that increases their own sense of power by putting someone down. It's not the relaxing, mind-opening humor we have been talking about.

The Emperor/General Paradigm guides not just the top leaders in an organization, but management all the way down, creating what Bob Basso calls the "give-orders-cover-your-tail-stay-on-people's-backs-till-the-job's-done" boss. Now, this kind of management has sometimes appeared to work in organizations where each role had well-defined, unchanging duties—in some military forces and old-fashioned factories, for instance. But in both subordinates and leaders, it promotes an "Us against Them" mentality, breeding distrust and even hostility on both sides. It also creates resentment in subordinates. People don't like to be treated as mere devices for achieving someone else's goals—that's the role of slaves or machines. The best that the Emperor/General manager can hope to get from workers is obedience—they'll do what they are told, but no more.

This kind of management also creates many problems. Because the paramount concern of authoritarian bosses is protecting their own power, they are suspicious of change and so do not adapt well in rapidly changing times like our own.

As Steve Wilson points out, too, when bosses show hostility and impatience, their negative energy gets passed on to workers in the form of stress. Morale is poor, there is little sense of teamwork, and communica-

tion is guarded rather than open. The manager is someone to be avoided, in extreme cases by calling in sick.[6]

Many of the problems created by authoritarian managers arise from their counterproductive attitude toward
failure and mistakes, which they cannot tolerate in either
their subordinates or themselves. A subordinate's failure
or mistake means that a command has not been carried
out; their own failure means weakness and so a lessen-
ing of their power.

When things don't go their way, their response is fear
or anger, either of which makes subordinates afraid of
making mistakes and so discourages risk-taking and
innovation. When subordinates do make mistakes, they
tend to avoid the boss' wrath by covering them up.
Broken equipment is quietly put back on the shelf rather
than tagged for repair. Reports of problems get shuffled
from desk to desk, wasting everyone's time, and making
the problems harder to fix when they are finally faced.

With this unhealthy attitude toward mistakes, neither
managers nor subordinates learn much, except how to
cover their tails and pass the buck. Someone who is
berated for making a mistake isn't in the open frame of
mind required for learning. The next time the problem
arises, the worker will feel anxious, but will not be better
prepared to handle it. Indeed, the stressful atmosphere
created by the fear of mistakes can *increase* the rate of
mistakes.

Humor Enhances the Effective Leader

In today's workplace, where adaptability to change,
risk-taking, creative problem-solving, and teamwork are
so important, we're changing our paradigm of the leader

to one that is more effective. *Fortune* magazine calls it "the new post-heroic leadership."[7] This is not to downplay the traits of traditional leaders which did work. New concepts of leadership should incorporate the best of the old concepts. And the traits—new and old—of effective leaders have strong connections with humor. Let's look at eleven of these traits.

Confidence

The first attribute of effective leaders is their confidence: they believe in their own abilities and the abilities of others in their organizations, and they act decisively and enthusiastically. This confidence is not complacency or unrealistic optimism. It is certainly not a self-delusory belief that they can't make mistakes or that there's no room for improvement. Some decisions made with confidence may turn out badly, but that doesn't mean that they should have been made timidly. It merely means that the failure should be faced honestly in order to correct it and move on.

Effective leaders don't waffle. They don't hide behind committees, consultants, and floods of memos to avoid criticism. They act decisively, and then take responsibility for their actions. While a weak leader plays simply not to lose, the effective leader plays to win.

In expressing confidence and building it in others, humor is invaluable. A witty quip at the right time shows a grasp of the situation as nothing else does. Self-effacing humor is especially good for expressing confidence. When you poke fun at your own shortcomings, you show that you can face problems squarely, without defensive illusions.

Control of the Situation

The confidence shown by effective leaders is not just a facade, but is based on their control of the situation. And here too there is a strong connection with humor. Think of the groups with whom you often meet. Who uses humor the most successfully? And who has the most control of what happens at those meetings?

The person who makes the group laugh steers the discussion and so the decisions. At Ford in the 1950s, there was a period when the accountants were running things. Projecting big losses, they had already shut down several plants. When they demanded another plant closing, Ford President Robert McNamara called a meeting of top executives. Most of them didn't want to close the plant, but no one could challenge the accountants' numbers. The argument for closing the plant seemed unbeatable, until one veteran executive bravely asked, "Why don't we close down *all* the plants and then we'll really start to save money?" There was laughter all around the table. With those few simple words, he had said more than volumes of economic data, and had expressed what everyone except the accountants were feeling. The top brass spared the plant, and decided that the accountants would no longer run the company.[8]

With humor, a leader can reframe a situation so that others look at it in a new way, and this reframing gives the leader control over their thinking. In the 1984 presidential campaign, incumbent Ronald Reagan faced Walter Mondale in three television debates. In the first, Reagan rambled and seemed confused. Many said afterward that at age 73, Reagan was too old for another term; some even suggested that he was in the early stages of Alzheimer's disease. So in the second debate someone asked him the inevitable question about the age issue. But his speechwriters had prepared a clever answer: "I am not going to make age an issue in this campaign. I am not going to exploit for political purposes my opponent's youth and inexperience." Everyone laughed, the age issue evaporated, and Reagan went on to win handsomely. He had given the impression of quick wit, and that made it look like he was still alert and bright.

An extreme example of the control which humor gives a speaker comes from Greenland, where until this century it was an important part of the legal system of the native people. Someone with a charge against another person—even murder—challenged that person to a verbal joust before the village. The two took turns taunting each other with exaggerated criticisms and sarcasm. In this kind of Don Rickles marathon, no attention was paid to the reasonableness of the claims. All that counted was who got the most laughs at the other's expense. That person was declared the winner, and the loser, if defeated badly, was ostracized from the community.

But humor does not have to put someone else down in order to give a leader control. When John Kennedy was criticized for nominating his brother as Attorney General, he defused the whole issue by saying, "I see nothing wrong with giving Robert some legal experience as Attorney General before he goes out to practice law." When under attack, even self-effacing humor can work. As long as it is humor you control, you still control the discussion. Consider the example cited earlier of Abraham Lincoln's sliding away from the charge of being two-faced, with the quip "If I had two faces, would I be wearing this one?"

Self-Control

Leaders have control not only of the situations they face, but of themselves. As the pressure increases, they do not succumb to fear or anger but are emotionally steady. Unless their problems are catastrophic, they don't swing from good days to bad days.

Humor is a big help in maintaining self-control, because, as we saw in Chapters 4 and 5, it blocks negative emotions. With the distance and perspective it provides, humor serves as a buffer against stressful events. That emotional steadiness spreads to the group, too, so that its members keep their cool. That's why bad news and decisions in crises are often announced with humor. When Winston Churchill went on the radio to tell the British people that Mussolini had come into World War II, he said it this way:

> The Italians have announced that they will
> fight on the Nazis' side. I think it's only fair.
> We had to put up with them last time.

In 1944 the German army had surrounded the U.S. 101st Airborne at Bastogne. When the German commander issued an ultimatum to surrender to U.S. General McAuliffe, the reply was one word—"Nuts!" That defiant quip reduced the stress among the American troops and strengthened their resolve to break through the German lines—which they went on to do.

Humility

The confidence of effective leaders is based not on self-glory or arrogance, but on humility. The direction of their thinking and concern is not inward but outward.

They see themselves as working not above the group, but in it. And when they exercise power, it is to benefit the group, not to flex their egos or increase their own status.

American business has seen too often what happens when leaders lack humility. Consider the reign of James L. Dutt as chairman of the $12.6-billion Beatrice companies in the early 1980s. He launched a $30-million corporate image ad campaign aimed largely at glorifying himself. He required that his picture be hung in every Beatrice office. He forced the corporate magazine to emphasize his exploits. Since he was a car collector and racing enthusiast, he committed $70 million of the company's money to sponsor a Formula I racing team, although Beatrice had no automotive product line. The more Dutt ruled like an emperor, the worse things got within the company. After more than three-quarters of top management had quit or been fired, he was finally booted out.[9] And his lack of humility was to blame for it all.

In cultivating and expressing humility, nothing works better than humor, especially self-effacing humor. In June 1962, as John Kennedy welcomed a group of students to Washington for summer jobs, he quipped, "Sometimes I wish I just had a summer job here." Instant rapport and solidarity! Suddenly the students saw him not as the most powerful man in the world, but as a former student who had moved on to a very hard job.

Kennedy's self-effacing humor made him look smart and on top of things, but at the same time humble and close to the people he led. When he began his presidency, everyone knew that he had won the election by a very narrow margin. So, addressing a group of five thousand in Chicago, he began:

> Some years ago in Fall River, Massachusetts, the mayor was elected by one vote, and every time he walked down the street, someone would say to him, "Say, I put you in office." I feel a little like that tonight. If all of you had voted the other way, I wouldn't be president.

The closest we have in recent politicians to Kennedy's humor is that of Mario Cuomo, former governor of New York. In his introduction to a speech at the New York Press Club, Cuomo mentioned some last-minute advice his wife Matilda had given him: "She said, 'I know it's a difficult subject and a tough group. But don't be intimidated. And don't try to be charming, witty, or intellectual. Just be yourself.'"[10] There is simply no better way to warm up an audience than that.

Self-effacing humor works for leaders because it expresses humility and confidence at the same time. It shows that you're aware of your limitations, but you have enough self-assurance to rise above them. Egoists don't use self-effacing humor. As Adlai Stevenson said, "Humor helps to distinguish the really bright and thoughtful, and also the humble . . . from the self-conscious and the self-righteous presumptuous type."

Mental Flexibility

Effective leaders do not plod along simply trying to maintain the status quo—they seize and even create opportunities. Especially today, they see change not as a threat but as the norm. Instead of the philosophy "If it ain't broke, don't fix it," they subscribe to what the Japanese call "kaizen," constant improvement. Even in successful times, they are looking for ways to make things better. Effective leaders are not locked into mental ruts, but can play with possible scenarios as easily as facts. They have imagination, which is an important part of their vision. In short, effective leaders are mentally flexible.

Humor, as we saw in Chapter 5, is connected with imagination, openness to novelty, and mental flexibility in general. The person with a good sense of humor sees something not just for what it is, but as the intersection of a large number of possibilities. Playing with possibilities is precisely the skill of comedians like Robin Williams and Jonathan Winters.

When leaders exercise their sense of humor, they not only cultivate their own mental flexibility, but bring out other people's mental flexibilty. Last year I participated in a program for the staff of a large hospital which was changing all its record-keeping from a problem-ridden computer system to a much better one. Although everyone hated the old system, they were naturally anxious about learning the new one. The CEO of the computer company understood that well, and had the imagination to use humor to make the transition smoother.

On the morning before the new system became operational, hospital staff assembled in the auditorium for a party. After coffee and Danish, the lights went down and through the doors came a New Orleans-style funeral procession, marching to a Dixieland dirge. The black casket they carried had the name of the old computer system painted on the side. At the front of the room they placed the casket onto a mound draped in black. The lead mourner gave a funny eulogy for the old computer system, complete with clips from old horror movies, and then they lowered the casket behind the mound. Just then the doors of the auditorium opened again and a very pregnant-looking woman waddled to the front of the room. "It's time, it's time," she cried. The lead mourner helped her walk behind the burial mound, where after a few seconds there was a loud baby's cry. Bursting through the front of the mound came a 170-lb. "baby" dressed only in a large diaper and bonnet—the CEO of the computer company. It took a long time for the laughter to subside, but when it did, he introduced himself and gave a great talk about how his new computer system would be like a new baby—something that the staff would love but would have to get used to. He also assured everyone that his company would provide expert training and would be on call to handle the inevitable glitches and misunderstandings.

Nothing in this man's job description had called for this kind of silliness, but its effect on the hospital staff was remarkable. In laughing, they relaxed, and later they had the memory of that CEO in diapers to recall whenever the computer system gave them trouble.

Constructive Attitude toward Mistakes

With their humility and mental flexibility, effective leaders show a willingness to take risks and a constructive attitude toward failure. Authoritarian leaders treat mistakes as punishable offenses, and so they avoid risks and discourage risk-taking in subordinates. But effective leaders see mistakes as part of learning and constant improvement, in both themselves and others. Instead of pretending to be infallible, they ask for criticism, admit their own mistakes, and are willing to change course. And they reward risk-taking and innovative ideas in others—even if they don't pan out. Progressive companies like 3M have long-standing policies that encourage creative risk-taking.

Some of the best advice about mistakes is found in Robert Townsend's *Further Up the Organization*[11]:

> Admit your own mistakes openly, maybe even joyfully.
>
> Encourage your associates to do likewise by commiserating with them. Never castigate. Babies learn to walk by falling down. If you beat a baby every time he falls down, he'll never care much for walking.
>
> My batting average on decisions at Avis was no better than .333. Two out of every three decisions I made were wrong. But my mistakes were discussed openly and most of them corrected with a little help from my friends.

Notice that even in writing about mistakes, Townsend shows his sense of humor. The best humor, as here, promotes a healthy attitude toward risk-taking and mistakes, because it sees all of us as in the same boat. It does not single out one person for mockery, but instead focuses on our common human condition, in which to avoid risk and mistakes is to stop growing.

Participation and Empowerment

A good leader is more coach than general, more *with* the group than *above* it. As Ross Perot said in his 1992 presidential campaign, leaders should serve their organizations, not the other way around.

Effective leaders make people feel like members of the team by being accessible to them, and showing, not just saying, that they care about them. They also minimize the number of levels of management and the status differences between those levels, because they know that a team can't be built out of people who feel unequal.

When they communicate, they are open and honest, and they prefer informal to formal interactions. As Townsend writes, "Real managers manage by frequent eyeball contact." He quotes one successful manager: "Half our meetings are held in the hall, the other half in the washroom."[12] Unlike authoritarian leaders, who don't want input from "the masses," effective leaders know the value of having as many different perspectives as possible, and they solicit them.

This style of leadership encourages a kind of participation which empowers not just their subordinates but the leaders themselves, because it puts the maximum number of people on their side, sharing their goals and moving with them. Without this sense of participation, subordinates may appear to go along, but their resentment is likely to come out in other ways. As Roger Smith, chairman of General Motors, commented, "You can't push people . . . you can't drag them. If they don't want to do something . . . they will stand there and smile at you, but there goes a red seat in a blue car."[13]

In fostering empowerment, participation, and consensus, few things work as well as humor, because it reduces distance between people and conveys the message "We're all in this together."

Self-effacing humor is an especially useful way for leaders to show that they are egalitarian and supportive. In calmly facing their own shortcomings and laughing at them, they show that they won't be shaken when others come to them with problems. That's why in his 1992 campaign Ross Perot poked fun not only at foreign lobbyists "in $1,000 alligator shoes," but at his own homeliness and humble origins. His humor was a perfect vehicle for the message "I'm just a regular person like you who is fed up with bad government. I'm not grabbing power for myself, but trying to give it back to you."

Knowledge

In contemporary organizations, the old saying that knowledge is power is truer than ever before. The corporation that thrives in the 21st century will be what Peter Senge calls "the learning corporation." Effective leaders are knowledge hungry, and they are seen as intelligent, clever, and "with it." In making decisions, they gather as much information as they can—not just facts and figures, but also subjective information on how people feel about issues. Unlike authoritarian managers, however, they do not hoard knowledge to increase their own power, but share information with their subordinates to empower them.

Humor is connected with knowledge in two ways. First, it is a good way for leaders to show their understanding of what's going on. When John Kennedy described Washington as "a city of Southern efficiency and Northern charm," for example, he sounded insightful. As Dorothy Parker said, "Wit has truth in it." Ronald Reagan's line quoted earlier about not making age an issue in the 1984 election dissolved the fear that he was getting senile, at least for those who didn't know that the quip had been prepared by a speechwriter.

Humor is also a useful device to reveal your knowledge of some potential problem without being heavy-handed about it. As we saw in Chapter 6, it can make your message non-threatening. Consider the factory manager mentioned in that chapter who wrote the memo at the beginning of baseball season:

Any employee desiring to be present at the death or funeral of a relative, please notify the foreman before 10 AM the day of the game.

The second connection of humor with knowledge is that the joking in an organization is a barometer of people's morale and concerns, and so to know the organization thoroughly, the wise leader pays attention to its current humor. In one stage of Kodak's downsizing, for instance, handbills started circulating which advertised a new movie starring Kodak's president and its CEO. It was entitled "Honey, I Shrunk the Company!" Copies were made from copies, until thousands were in circulation. Company leaders could not afford to ignore the anxiety underlying that humor.

At the University of Montana, one department head put up a bulletin board for jokes in his office, offering a cash prize for the best joke each week. A vice president at a data management firm in Fort Washington, Pennsylvania installed a blackboard for people to write graffiti. Both got easy access to problems they wouldn't otherwise have known about.

Clearheadedness

In their thinking and communicating, effective leaders are objective and realistic. Their confidence and enthusiasm are based not on wishful thinking, but on clear goals and sound judgment.

Humor promotes clearheaded thought and communication. As we have seen, it gives you distance and perspective, getting you outside your own point of view. That allows you to see yourself and your situation objectively, and so to think straight. Leaders who express themselves with humor, too, look like they have a clear understanding of what's going on. The best wit goes straight to the heart of an issue, cutting through confusion and self-deception. As Leon Harris has pointed out, it is impossible to be witty vaguely or generally.

Appreciation of Complexity

Effective leaders look beneath the surface of events. They do not think in black-and-white terms, but acknowledge the complexity and ambiguity of situations. They also appreciate the diversity of perspectives possible on any situation. Unlike authoritarian leaders, who consider disagreement a mark of disloyalty, flexible leaders welcome diverse perspectives, and learn as much as they can from people who disagree with them.

This ability to see things in depth and from several perspectives is part of creativity and innovation. It is also an important skill in eliciting the best from other people, since it encourages them to express themselves openly. In showing that they see the various sides of an issue, too, leaders can handle sensitive situations with grace and fairness, minimizing possible offense, and at the same time achieving their goals.

Humor is useful here, because it fosters the ability to see things in their complexity and from many perspectives. It is also a non-threatening way to get other people to see things from your point of view. Barry Goldwater, long-time Senator from Arizona, told how his application to join the Phoenix Country Club was rejected because his father was Jewish. He handled the situation by calling the president of the country club to ask a simple question: "Since I'm only half-Jewish, can I join if I only play nine holes?" He was quickly admitted.

When Eugene Cafiero was president of Chrysler, he flew to England to visit a troubled auto plant. He was met by a group of hostile union men, one of whom introduced himself loudly, "I'm Eddie McClusky and I'm a Communist." Cafiero enthusiastically put out his hand and said, "How do you do. I'm Gene Cafiero and I'm a Presbyterian." Everyone relaxed and laughed—the two now understood each other.[14]

Critical Thinking

The last leadership trait we'll relate to humor is critical thinking. Effective leaders do not take things at face value, but ask lots of questions, and evaluate what they see and hear.

Thinking critically is hard. It takes effort and time; and when it turns up confusion, pretense, or outright deception, it threatens those caught in the act. The philosopher Bertrand Russell wasn't far off the mark when he said, "Most people would sooner die than think. In fact they do so." But effective leaders realize that critical thinking is essential to their role.

They also foster it in others. Instead of being overly reverent toward the powers that be, they encourage careful questioning of authority, including their own. Sycophantic subordinates who rubber-stamp their ideas wouldn't take them beyond where they are already, and wouldn't save them from foolish blunders.

This questioning of authority goes hand in hand with humor, as we can see in editorial cartoons and other political humor, and in much of the humor that circulates in the workplace. Laughter expresses a healthy refusal to accept authority figures as infallible.

More generally, critical thinking and humor go together. Consider what comedians do. They critically analyze the world around them—family life, advertising, entertainment, politics, etc.—looking for incongruity. And most incongruity comes in the form of problems and vices. That's why for thousands of years the stock characters in comedy have been the fool, the liar, the blowhard, etc.

The critical thinking that comes with humor is especially valuable in resisting our natural human tendency toward "Groupthink," a word coined by Irving Janis for the way a group's desire to achieve unanimity keeps its members from examining what they are agreeing with.[15] Groupthink often occurs under a charismatic leader. A good example of the damage it does is the infamous Bay of Pigs invasion of 1961. Kennedy had inherited from Eisenhower a deeply flawed plan to invade Cuba with only a few thousand troops. Instead of looking at the plan with a fresh critical eye, Kennedy just went along with it; after all, Eisenhower had been a general before becoming president. Worse, Kennedy's advisers simply went along with him; they didn't even sketch possible scenarios for the invasion and imagine what could go wrong. In rubber-stamping the plan, they did their president and their country a deep disservice, not a favor. If they had played devil's advocate, putting the plan in the worst possible light, even making fun of it as, say, George Carlin might, Kennedy would have realized its serious flaws and would not have approved it.

It is because authoritarian leaders like Hitler, Stalin, and Ayatollah Khomeini demanded groupthink that they discouraged critical thinking and humor. They were especially lacking in a sense of humor about themselves, because they couldn't see themselves objectively. Any mentally flexible leader, by contrast, will not want irrational allegiance and will appreciate the critical spirit of humor.

That's why, since the days of the pharoahs, there have been court jesters, who poke fun at leaders, not just to amuse them but to keep them, and everyone else, on their toes. A friend of mine who works for a large Canadian bank told me of a contemporary use of court jester humor to encourage critical thinking. Like many large corporations, his bank has a monthly in-house TV program, on which the CEO discusses trends and policies, and answers questions from employees. But unlike many corporate TV programs, this one does not present the CEO as infallible. In one segment, next to the CEO appears a puppet who asks tough questions and pokes fun at the CEO for past mistakes. The humor here gives employees permission to think for themselves about problems and procedures at the bank. That makes them feel more involved in the corporation, improves their effectiveness, and thus benefits the bank.

In the U.S. the closest we've had to a national court jester was Will Rogers, whose humor brought out serious problems without getting mean-spirited. "At some time, senators and congress people will have to retire and return home to make an honest living like everyone else" is a classic Rogers quip. He was a frequent guest at the White House. After being introduced to President Calvin Coolidge, Rogers said, "Sorry, I didn't catch the name." The president laughed heartily—a good sign. Coolidge, despite his reputation for being dour, appreciated the ability of humor to keep people out of mental ruts. Every once in a while, he would press all the buttons on his desk and then hide behind the door, as aides, generals, and Secret Service people came running in. "I just wanted to see whether you were doing your job," he would explain laughing.

Humor's critical spirit makes it a powerful weapon against the pomposity, gobbledegook, and red tape that encumber any bureaucracy. For years Senator William Proxmire gave his "Golden Fleece" Award to those who had pulled expensive scams on the federal government. The Navy, for example, had a contract with McDonnell Douglas for ordinary threaded nuts (13¢ each in hardware stores) that were described as "hexiform rotatable surface compression units" and sold for $2,043.00 apiece!

In the same critical spirit, Jim Boren, President of the International Association of Professional Bureaucrats, created a sculpture of a featherless bird, which he presented along with a certificate inducting the recipient into "The Order of the Bird." This award, or more often the threat of its conferral, has gotten many bureaucrats moving. In 1969, for example, a man in a Naval Hospital had his spinal cord injured by a surgeon's slip-up, and lost use of his legs. Dozens of bureaucrats delayed settlement of his case for nine years. Boren decided that people who could shuffle the man's claim back and forth that long deserved public recognition. So he wrote to the Department of Labor announcing that pending the final approval of twenty-nine committees, they would be receiving "The Order of the Bird" with full press coverage. Within ten days the nine-year-old claim was miraculously approved.

Managing with Humor

A sense of humor, as we have seen, is valuable not just for presidents and heads of corporations, but for anyone who leads or supervises people. Managers at all levels can be more effective by incorporating humor into their workplaces. Here are a few suggestions for putting more humor into yours.

1. Lead by example. Lighten up; show more than your "executive cool" face; let others see that you have a full range of human emotions.

2. Integrate humor into your speeches, presentations, memos, and letters. When you're commending someone, say, or even delivering a negative message, add a touch of humor and watch for the difference it makes.

3. Look more relaxed and approachable by using self-effacing humor. If you have framed credentials hanging on your office wall, add to them the lifetime warranty on your new muffler—in a walnut frame with gold trim.

4. When you are hiring managers, use as criteria their humor, imagination, enthusiasm, and their ability to spark all these in other people.

5. In meetings, use humor to set a relaxed tone, stir up creative thinking, and defuse conflicts.

6. Have a bulletin board for funny and fun items; better yet, let these be put up on regular bulletin boards. When people go on vacation, encourage them to send postcards for the bulletin board—regular tourist cards, or even better, goofy and tacky postcards, like the giant trout attacking the boat. Get the ball rolling by sending the first card when you go on vacation.

In one university where I taught, there was a bulletin board near the office of the writing program. One day people spontaneously started putting up examples of mangled prose, gobbledegook, and other bad writing. Many of the items were memos from our own university administrators. Then someone started a list of redundant phrases, including:

free gift	small speck
dangerous threat	qualified experts
human error	exciting adventure
advance planning	duplicate copy.

Soon there was also a running list of oxymorons—phrases that sound contradictory:

non-working mother	military intelligence
industrial park	jumbo shrimp
pretty ugly	civil war
American cheese	Great Britain.

Before long everyone, including administrators, was checking the board regularly, and adding to it. Not only was this fun, but everyone's writing improved.

7. Plan fun changes of pace into the day and week. In Hawaii the last day of the work week is designated "Aloha Friday" and people come to work in casual, colorful clothes. That informality pays off; for most Hawaiian businesses, Friday is the most productive workday. On the mainland, at the end of 1994, two-thirds of major employers allowed casual wear at least occasionally. Of these, 81 percent said that relaxing dress restrictions improved morale, and 47 percent said it increased productivity.[16]

A simple break suggested by Bob Basso is a Trash Party. Call time out. The next five minutes are for throwing out papers, cleaning out files, and straightening up desks. Tom Peters recommends the ritual of spring cleaning: "For two days, everyone dons 501s and specially printed T-shirts and cleans house—toss out old files, clear the fridge, do whatever it takes to induce the feeling of a fresh start."[17] Once in a while bring an instant camera to work and take a five-minute break for a few group shots. Let people pose any way they like, and then put the pictures on the bulletin board.

Have occasional theme days when people are invited (not compelled) to come in appropriate attire. The possibilities are endless—Dress Down Day, 50s Day, 60s Day, 70s Day, Nerd/Nerdette Day, Polyester Day, etc.

For more ideas on activities to break up the day, week, and year, and other ways to incorporate humor into management, see Bob Basso and Judi Klosek's book *This Job Should Be Fun,* Ron Garland's *Making Work Fun,* and Steve Wilson's *The Art of Mixing Work and Play.*

General Lessons for Managers

In exploring the connections between humor, leadership, and management, some general principles have emerged. We can close this chapter by spelling them out in more detail.

The central principle is that people do their best work in an atmosphere where they have control over their work and feel like valued members of a team. There are several ways to create this atmosphere. Let's consider six of the most important.

1. Make the physical environment comfortable. The most basic way we show people that we value them is by attending to their basic needs. When a guest comes to our house, it is simple courtesy to make sure the place—especially the dining room and the bathroom—is clean, and to offer them something good to eat and

drink. But many workplaces pay little attention to such things as where and what people will eat, and the adequacy of the restrooms. The unspoken message to workers is that they are not respected as people.

Besides making sure that the basic facilities are adequate and clean, you should give some thought to how the place looks. If it hasn't been redecorated since Nixon resigned, consider doing that. Ask people to vote on what's the biggest eyesore in the place, then remove the "winner." In fact, it's smart to change anything that gets more than a few votes.

You might even consider decorating with a sense of fun, especially if creativity is important in your business. One advertising agency in Venice, California, for example, set up its 50,000-square-foot "warehouse office" with no lobby or standard reception area, but instead "Main Street," an open space with vintage cars, an employee art gallery, and a giant silver whale. Off Main Street is a big conference room shaped like a fish. To stress equality, the conference table is an irregular shape with no head or foot. Outside the building is a pirate flag.

How does this playful atmosphere affect workers, management, and clients? The firm was voted Agency of the Decade by *Advertising Age* magazine, and it has gone from zero billing to $1.2 billion in 23 years.[18]

2. Reduce the psychological distance between management and non-management. To do that, reduce hierarchy to as few levels as possible. Minimize formality. Make it easy and comfortable for people to meet with you and each other.

The authoritarian way many managers treat subordinates creates an "Us against Them" atmosphere that is counterproductive and expensive. Lawsuits by workers cost employers over $20 billion a year in attorneys' fees alone—added to that are the settlements and judgments. According to a recent survey of corporate attorneys, the main source of these lawsuits is the frontline supervisor, who does not try to work out problems but instead gets hostile.[19]

3. Involve people in decision-making that affects them. At the very least, ask for their opinions. Those who are part of a decision-making process have a personal investment in what comes out of that process. People who are simply given orders, on the other hand, often resist management. One of the most expensive ways they do that is by wasting time. According to a *New York Times* report, the deliberate waste of time in the workplace costs American business $170 billion annually.[20]

4. Foster camaraderie and team spirit. Get to know your people, greet them by name, and schedule events where they can get to know each other. Make all of this as egalitarian as possible.

One of the most basic ways we have of getting to know each other is sharing food and drink. At Versatec, a Silicon Valley firm, whenever an employee, regardless of rank, celebrates a five-year service anniversary, Renn Zaphiropoulos, the CEO, takes him or her to lunch. At Ben and Jerry's Ice Cream, many of the activities of the joy committee center around food. One night at ten o'clock they served breakfast for the second and third shifts; another time they concocted the world's largest milkshake.

If these methods of fostering team spirit aren't feasible in your workplace, how about bringing in coffee and donuts on Monday morning, or arranging a picnic lunch in a nearby park? How about putting small coffee makers in each work area, or hot-air popcorn machines?

5. Use positive rather than negative reinforcement, whenever possible. Any group works better on enthusiasm, desire, and other positive energy, than on fear, resentment, and negative energy.

When you do have to bring up something negative, focus on what can be done to improve it, and ask for ideas on improvement. Never make a criticism sound like an attack on the person—it's the behavior you should be concerned with. Don't try to make people feel guilty, or rub their noses in what they've done wrong. Vindictiveness may make you feel triumphant for thirty seconds, but it's likely to make people resent you for years. That's no way to improve their performance. Worse, it will shut down whatever channels of communication you had with them.

Bob Basso suggests prefacing a criticism with two positive comments, and following it with another positive comment, along with a word of encouragement at the end. And even the criticism, he says, should be phrased in a non-threatening way, such as "I wish WE could find a way to solve the problem of_____."[21] One place to emphasize positive reinforcement is in performance reviews. Don't treat the criticisms as the real purpose of the review, and just squeak out one or two vague positive comments at the beginning. Come up with as many good things to say about the person as you can. And be specific. Employees will appreciate your noticing their work and will be in a positive mood to hear about the areas in which they need to improve.

Unfortunately, many managers have operated as cops rather than coaches for so long that they don't realize how negative they sound, and what a damper they put on other people's enthusiasm, willingness to take risks, and creativity in general. No one is likely to be innovative under a manager who responds to every new idea by shooting it down, or "firehosing" it, to use Robert Kreigel's word.

Kriegel has devised a clever way to show people how negative their thinking may be, and to help them overcome this tendency. At a brainstorming session for a health-care organization, he put a loaded squirt gun in the middle of the table and told the group to use it on anyone who "firehosed" an idea. A few minutes into the session, as a vice president made a negative remark, he stopped mid-sentence, grabbed the gun and squirted himself between the eyes. That opened the floodgates, and soon the water was flying everywhere. After about half an hour, however, as people became attuned to the harmful effects of negative remarks, their whole approach changed. Instead of trying to tear down each other's ideas, they started supporting and building on them. The experience was liberating, and that brainstorming session led to the development of a line of very successful products. This group now puts squirt guns out at all its meetings, just in case.[22]

6. Encourage people to take risks and try new things. That's a big part of empowerment—people can't be empowered to just follow the book! And when what they try doesn't work, treat what happened not as a regrettable failure, but as a learning experience.

The six principles we have been discussing are good for empowering people as team members. But in the contemporary workplace, where change is the rule and we are looking for constant improvement, we have to go further. We have to encourage people to constantly re-evaluate situations, looking at them from new perspectives.

Some of today's most successful organizations got that way not by following conventional practices, but by looking at things from fresh perspectives. Consider The Body Shop, the British cosmetics company. Its founder, Anita Roddick, did not have traditional business training, and so began without the usual preconceptions. In an industry built largely on advertising and fancy packaging, Roddick does not advertise at all, but relies on word-of-mouth, and her products come in refillable bottles originally designed to collect urine specimens. Instead of expensive market research, The Body Shop has a well-used suggestion box in each store. The annual reports are printed on postcards. As a personal principle, Roddick is sensitive to the environmental effects of her company. Many of her products are made with banana oil, and pressing that oil leaves tons of banana skins. So figuring out a way to turn the skins into paper, she set up a paper manufacturing plant in Nepal and then turned over the plant to the local community. Breaking with tradition in all these ways, The Body Shop has become the largest and most profitable cosmetics company in Great Britain. Without advertising, its logo is more widely known in England than the Golden Arches of McDonald's are in the U.S.[23]

The lesson for all organizations here is to be open to all kinds of perspectives, especially unconventional ones. You can get ideas from all divisions and levels of your organization. Even better is to have them giving each other ideas. That's why more than half of the Fortune 1,000 companies now use "superteams" to solve problems and create new products. Superteams include people from sales, manufacturing, marketing, finance, engineering, etc., who might otherwise be competing in turf wars, but instead are cooperating. They see things from many different angles at once, and together come up with ideas that no single division would have produced.

A particularly effective way to get people from different divisions to see things from each others' perspectives is to rotate their roles. It provides a welcome change of pace and can lead to useful suggestions. People gain knowledge and skills, and that is empowering. They're more able to see the big picture and identify with the whole organization, rather than just their area. And they become then more sympathetic with other departments, which reduces conflict.

In the fall of 1984, the city government of Long Beach, California rotated all of its managers for a day. After that, cooperation between departments improved greatly. An unexpected benefit to staff members was that the transplanted managers had to politely ask them for help. They loved being able to take charge and make suggestions that were appreciated.[24]

In the late 1980s, the Sarasota, Florida store in the Lechmere chain used job rotation to deal with labor shortages. They offered pay raises to employees for learning extra jobs. Cashiers, for example, learned to drive forklifts in the warehouse. With this more versatile workforce, the store can now quickly adjust to changes in staffing needs, and it is substantially more productive than other stores in the chain.[25]

You can also learn from clients and their perspectives. Market research is the traditional technique here, but there are many others. One is to consider how customers *mis*use a product, to see what new possibilities it might have. Observing how people used the crates designed for oranges and for milk cartons, for example, to hold other things, entrepreneurs began marketing them as storage containers for such things as sound recordings and file folders. Kitty litter was invented when someone noticed a cat "visiting" a open bag of gravel designed for cleaning up grease and oil.

To get new perspectives, it can also be enlightening to put managers into the customer's shoes. When there was a drop in sales at Harley-Davidson Motorcycles a few years ago, the CEO had all senior management make cross country trips on Harleys, go to bikers' rallies, and get to see things through the eyes of their customers, including the Hell's Angels. One thing they learned quickly was that most bikers modify their motorcycles with a chopped chassis, a sculpted gas tank, etc. When the executives got back to headquarters, they incorporated some of the more popular custom features into the new models, and profitability and market share increased handsomely.

An even more dramatic practitioner of this switching technique is Barbara Sabol. As New York City's welfare commissioner in 1992, she spent nine months in the worn shoes of her one million clients. Putting on wigs and scarves and carrying false identification, the $110,000-a-year manager went around to welfare and unemployment offices to see the whole operation from below. She was sent to the wrong line and the wrong address, she ran into lots of red tape as she tried to get work, and she was scolded and mocked by a social worker. "I ceased to be," she commented, "nobody saw my spark." What she found was disturbing, but it changed her whole approach to her organization.

Robert Townsend suggests an easier way to put yourself in the client's shoes—"CALL YOURSELF UP."

> When you're off on a business trip or a vacation, pretend you're a customer. Telephone some part of your organization and ask for help. You'll run into some real horror shows. Don't blow up and ask for name, rank, and serial number: you're trying to correct, not punish. If it happens on a call to the Dubuque office, just suggest to the manager (through channels, dummy) that he make a few test calls for himself.
>
> Then try calling yourself up and see what indignities you've built into your own defenses.[26]

It can also be helpful for managers from one business to change their perspective by looking at a related business. Robert Kriegel was working with a group of hospital administrators, trying to get them to understand how to cater to their clients. He suggested that they go on separate week-long cruises to see what it's like to receive total service. Eight administrators did, and came back with a combined list of over a hundred improvements to make in their hospitals. Fresh flowers were added to hallways, a greeter was put in the lobby, and clearer information was provided to patients and their families. As one administrator described the improvements, they helped "put 'hospitality' back in 'hospital.'"[27]

Now traditional authoritarian managers would probably balk at the idea of sending people on cruises, as well as having them switch jobs or squirt each other across a

226

conference table. They'd also reject my suggestions for building more humor and fun into organizations. Let's cut out the frivolous nonsense, they'd say, and get back to *work*, as we did in the good old days.

Just how good the old days actually were, is open to discussion, but one thing is certain—they were the *old* days. Things have changed irreversibly, and will continue to change with increasing speed. Sweatshops run according to the Philosophy of the Third Little Pig are obsolete. Today, seeing things from the customer's perspective, having workers identify with the whole operation, building horizontal teams rather than power hierarchies, cultivating mental flexibility, and using humor to do all these things, are not fads. They are survival techniques for making it into the 21st century.

Notes

[1] Steve Wilson, *The Art of Mixing Work and Play* (Columbus, OH: Applied Humor Systems, 1992), p. 60; and P. Buhler, "Wanted: Humor in the Workplace," *Supervision* 52 (1991), pp.21-23.

[2] AP report cited in Steve Wilson, *The Art of Mixing Work and Play* (Columbus, OH: Applied Humor Systems, 1992), p. 17.

[3] Tom Peters, *Thriving on Chaos* (New York: Knopf, 1988), p. 462.

[4] Ibid., p. 475.

[5] Robert Townsend, *Up the Organization* (New York: Alfred A. Knopf, 1970), p. 199.

[6] Steve Wilson, *The Art of Mixing Work and Play* (Columbus, OH: Applied Humor Systems, 1992), pp. 94-95.

[7] *Fortune,* cover story, Feb. 21, 1994.

[8] Mark McCormack, *What They Don't Teach You at Harvard Business School* (New York: Bantam, 1984), pp. 46-47.

[9] Michael E. McGill, *American Business and the Quick Fix* (New York: Henry Holt, 1988), pp. 91-92.

10 Malcolm Kushner, *Lighten Up: How to Use Humor for Business Success* (New York: Simon and Schuster, 1990), p. 81.

11 Robert Townsend, *Further Up the Organization* (New York: Harper and Row, 1984), p. 141.

12 Ibid., p.161.

13 *Fortune,* Aug. 18, 1986, p. 27.

14 Walter Kiechell III, "Executives Ought to be Funnier," *Fortune,* December 12, 1983, p. 206.

15 Irving L. Janis, *Groupthink* (Boston: Houghton Mifflin, 1972).

16 Survey of 750 major employers conducted by Campbell Research Corp., reported in *St. Petersburg Times,* September 30, 1994, 10 H.

17 Tom Peters, *The Pursuit of Wow! Every Person's Guide to Topsy-Turvy Times* (New York: Vintage, 1994), p. 57.

18 Bob Basso and Judi Klosek, *This Job Should Be Fun* (Holbrook MA: Bob Adams, 1991), p. 178.

19 Ibid., p.129.

20 *NY Times,* May 14, 1989. Business sec. 2.

21 Bob Basso and Judi Klosek, *This Job Should Be Fun* (Holbrook MA: Bob Adams, 1991), p. 137.

22 Robert Kriegel, *If it ain't broke . . . BREAK IT!* (New York: Warner, 1991), pp. 30-31.

23 Ibid., pp.108-109.

24 Bob Basso and Judi Klosek, *This Job Should Be Fun* (Holbrook MA: Bob Adams, 1991), p. 118.

25 *Inc.,* July 1989, p. 53.

26 Robert Townsend, *Further Up the Organization* (New York: Harper and Row, 1984), p. 25.

27 Robert Kriegel, *If it ain't broke . . . BREAK IT!* (New York: Warner, 1991), pp. 151-152.

WHEN IT'S WRONG TO LAUGH

Negative Humor

In exploring the many benefits of humor in the workplace, we have concentrated on positive humor. But for a complete picture of how humor fits into our work and into our lives generally, we need to say something about negative humor.

By negative humor I do not mean humor that happens to focus on something negative, such as mistakes, failure, or misfortune. *Most* humor does that, and when the attitude is not negative and the humor doesn't have a negative effect on people, it's not negative humor. When people joke after a flood, for example, as a way of coming together and coping with the disaster, their humor is positive. When Thomas Edison joked with his employees about their thousands of false starts in inventing the light bulb, that humor kept them going and was positive.

In calling some humor negative, I mean that it involves a negative attitude toward people and has a negative effect on them. Such humor may do physical harm, as some practical jokes do, or more often, psychological harm, as in wisecracks that focus on mistakes in a humiliating, discouraging way. In contrast to Edison's positive humor, consider the belittling sarcasm some bosses crank out whenever a mistake is made. Instead of feeling uplifted, people feel like quitting their jobs. Or consider the difference between good-natured kidding, which promotes solidarity, and the obscene joking involved in a lot of sexual harassment.

Between positive and negative humor, there is a difference in attitude toward life as a whole. Positive humor embodies an open-minded, experimental approach to life that delights in new perspectives and possibilities, while negative humor rejects what is new or different. Those who mocked the newly-invented automobile and airplane, for example, engaged in negative humor. Racist jokes, similarly, don't open people's minds to other groups, but instead reject those groups.

The difference in attitude between positive and negative humor makes a big difference in the way people feel about each other. While positive humor comes from caring, negative humor comes from fear, distrust, or outright hostility. Positive humor brings us together and lets everyone feel good; negative humor singles out victims whom we turn against. So while positive humor builds morale and team spirit, negative humor tears them down.

Negative humor may have the veneer of fun, but underneath are feelings of distrust, fear, and envy. Sigmund Freud, the founder of psychiatry, pointed out that jokes can be a way of expressing emotions we are not allowed to express directly. If there is a group of people whom we would like to physically attack, for example, but laws against violence won't let us, then we might tell nasty jokes about that group being stupid or lazy, as a way of releasing our aggression.

In much negative humor, jokers' negative feelings come from their own sense of inadequacy. They put other people down in order to make themselves feel better. The philosopher Thomas Hobbes said that laughter occurs most often in people "that are conscious of the fewest abilities in themselves; who are forced to keep themselves in their own favor by observing the imperfections of other[s]."[1] Now Hobbes believed that *all* humor was competitive, which, as we have seen, is not the case. But we can understand his point for humor that *is* competitive. People who are always putting others down are probably none too sure of themselves.

One place to see how jokes substitute for more direct forms of aggression is in politics. Political candidates are not allowed to get physically hostile, but they can make nasty jokes to put each other down. In the last decade, many American political leaders have even used scornful name-calling as a substitute for political debate. Instead of presenting a careful justification for bombing Libya in 1986, for example, President Reagan called Libyan leader Muammar al-Qaddafi names like "Looney Tunes" and "Mad Dog." In the Fall of 1992, J. Peter Grace, CEO of W.R. Grace and Co., was the guest of honor at the dedication of a new factory in Milwaukee. In his speech he referred to New York Governor Mario Cuomo as "Cuomo the Homo," and New York City Mayor David Dinkins as "Dinkins the Pinkins." Around that time George Bush was giving campaign speeches in which he mockingly called Vice-Presidential candidate Al Gore "Ozone Man" for having written a book about the need to preserve the environment.

A Mostly Male Phenomenon

To understand where negative humor like this comes from, and how to avoid it, we need to look into the differences between men's humor and women's humor.

Hostile humor is based on a combative, win-lose approach to human relationships that comes largely from male aggressiveness. The biological drive here is the same one that attracts men to bullfighting, boxing, and war; its physical source is the male hormone, testosterone.

The natural aggressiveness of male humor shows most clearly in pranks and practical jokes, which cause inconvenience and even suffering to their victims. A trench digger in Florida, for example, shouted "Snake!" as he threw a vine at a co-worker. The man had a heart attack. A watchman in Louisiana died of a heart attack after he was "kidnapped" by co-workers as a joke.[2]

A milder example of male aggressive humor is the game of "playing the dozens" among African-American young men. The two sides trade insults until one loses by getting flustered and angry. A similar kind of humor has dominated American television for over twenty years. Since "All in the Family," sitcoms have consisted largely of family members and co-workers trading insults. The basic laugh-getter is the sarcastic put-down. When the lines are delivered by female characters like Murphy Brown (Candice Bergen), the humor is often unconvincing, because the sarcasm is decidedly male.

Since we want to understand male humor, and most humor occurs in conversation, we should say something about how males operate in conversation. Because they are concerned with power and control, males are more aggressive in conversation than females. They enjoy taking center stage, and getting the best of others. Females tend to be more cooperative and supportive of others in conversation, as in life generally. That's why women apologize much more often than men. When men and women are talking together, men usually take the lead.[3] They also interrupt women more often than women interrupt them.

Now producing humor is one way of exercising power in a conversation. To be telling the jokes and making the wisecracks is to control the conversation. So it's natural that male assertiveness and dominance in conversation often take the form of humor.

It was as children that we all learned how to fit into conversations, and into exchanges involving humor. Traditionally boys learned to take charge in conversations, while girls learned to be good listeners. Boys were rewarded for being funny; girls were socialized to appreciate humor but not to produce it. A young boy whose clowning made adults laugh was "a little entertainer"; a girl who tried to be funny in the same ways was "making a spectacle of herself."

As adolescents, girls were discouraged from being funny, especially with boys. The advice to girls in a 1972 book, *Teen Scene—1001 Groovy Hints and Tips*, is still not out of date: "You may be a quick wit with your friends, but cool it when he's around." On a date the girl, and later the woman, was supposed to be the recipient of the humor, and of the conversation generally, as she was the recipient of the dinner and the movie. Her overall role was to support the male and enhance his self-esteem.

Often she might not find his humor funny, just as she didn't always find his football stories interesting, but she would learn to fake laughter, as she learned to fake interest in his stories, and would later learn to fake orgasms. That's why so much female laughter came out as forced giggles. Its message to the male was "See, I'm enjoying myself—honestly!"[4]

Since producing humor in a conversation is a power role, men saw women who were actively funny, instead of just an audience for their humor, as threatening, much like women who could flip them in judo class. So when a woman got a lot of laughs, her humor was written off either as silly giggling, or if she was clever and cynical, as bitchiness. This bias against funny women is not limited to our country, by the way. In many cultures, women who tell jokes, or even laugh too loud, are seen as sexually promiscuous.

Traditional humor supported male power not only in the way it put males center stage and females in the audience, but also in its content. A lot of traditional jokes put females down, portraying them as empty-headed, manipulative, or as merely sexual objects—anything but rational and equal to men. One of the most popular joke-types of the 1950s, for example, was the mother-in-law joke. But have you ever heard a father-in-law joke? Today mother-in-law jokes are out, but we still have comedians like Andrew Dice Clay who have built lucrative careers on women-bashing.

Sexist jokes, like racist jokes, were part of the "old boy" network, which promoted white male solidarity by keeping women and minority groups "in their place." When women protested against sexist jokes, men quickly tried to deflect the criticism with lines like "Can't you take a joke?" and "Don't you have a sense of humor?"

The anti-female attitude of much traditional humor, along with men's unwillingness to let women produce humor in conversation, kept all but a few women out of the comedy most similar to conversation, stand-up comedy. The women who did become stand-up comics usually made themselves and other women the target of their joking, in order to reduce the potential threat to men. Phyllis Diller was acceptable, because her tangled bleached hair made her look electrocuted, and most of her jokes were about being a lousy wife. Joan Rivers got laughs by talking about how far her breasts and buttocks had sagged, and by making fun of Queen Elizabeth, Elizabeth Taylor, and other women. There was no female counterpart to Lenny Bruce, Mort Sahl, George Carlin, or even Bob Newhart.

In the last twenty years, fortunately, traditional sexism has been declining in American culture. As women have come to a sense of their own value, they have taken a more active role in humor and conversation, and have begun to take their rightful place in business and the professions. As Regina Barreca comments, they have discovered that "the traits supposedly reserved for a guy— such as intelligence, ambition, economic acumen, and a sense of humor— were in fact all the factors that added up to winning in the workplace."[5]

The blossoming of women's humor can be seen in stand-up comedy, where Joy Behar, Elayne Boosler, Susie Essman, Carol Leifer, Rita Rudner, Judy Tenuta, and dozens of other women comedians (no longer "comediennes") now draw the same crowds as their male colleagues. Women no longer have to make fun of themselves to get a laugh. In fact, much of their humor shows up the irrationality and unfairness of traditional sexism.

They do poke fun at themselves, but not in the old Joan Rivers style of self-mockery. Rita Rudner, for example, talks about wanting to have children but being scared by the stories she's heard of childbirth.

> One of my friends told me that she was in labor for *36 hours*. I don't even want to do something that *feels good* for 36 hours.

She's laughing at herself here, but her humor is full of savvy. Or consider Rudner's explanation of sexual problems:

> I just read that men reach their sexual peak at 18. Women reach their sexual peak at 35. Do you get the feeling that God is into practical jokes? We're reaching our sexual peak right around the same time they're discovering they have a favorite chair.

Women's Humor as Positive Humor

The kind of humor that is emerging today from women (and from an encouraging number of men) is quite different from traditional male aggressive humor. In fact, it has the positive features of the humor we have been discussing throughout this book.

One of the best examinations of this humor is Regina Barreca's *They Used to Call Me Snow White . . . But I Drifted: Women's Strategic Use of Humor*. I'd like to pick out three features of women's humor that she discusses.

First, women's humor is cooperative rather than competitive. It is not a contest of individual performances, but a group exploration of issues of common concern. When women hear a funny story, they don't try to top it. Their response is rather, "Oh, thank God, that happened to you, too! It means I'm not crazy!"

Second, women's humor usually arises from issues in their lives, rather than from rhetorical flair or mere verbal cleverness. That's why they typically tell funny stories about themselves and their friends, rather than fictional jokes. It's often said that women don't tell jokes very well, but there's a good reason for that: they usually don't remember bits of fiction that are irrelevant to their lives.

Third, women's humor usually doesn't work by finding a victim to humiliate, especially a helpless victim. It isn't ridicule of someone's failure or suffering. That's why most women don't play practical jokes and why they detest "The Three Stooges." Macho wisecracks like Clint Eastwood's line in *Dirty Harry*, "Make my day," make women feel uncomfortable rather than amused.

This is not to say that women's humor never involves conflict or has a target. But when there is a target, it is the powerful rather than the weak. And what is criticized is less the person than that person's objectionable attitude or behavior. Women's humor with a target is not competitive mockery but a way of spotlighting issues.

In some situations of conflict, women's humor gently gets everyone out of an embarrassing situation. Consider the women who noticed a male colleague at meetings dropping his pen under the table, so that he could bend down and look at their legs. Instead of confronting him or filing a complaint, they simply got ready for the next meeting by printing on their knees "HI RALPH," one letter per kneecap. His peek that day was his last.[6]

But women also use humor to wake people up to their own prejudices. Connie Chung, who became co-anchor of the CBS evening news, rose rapidly in the television news business. At one job, a male co-worker asked her whether it was being a Chinese woman that had gotten her promoted so quickly. Instead of getting upset, she did his racism and sexism one better. Pointing to a senior vice president across the room, she said, "Yes. Bill likes the way I do his shirts."

Women aren't the only ones who face insensitive questions, of course. Jazz pianist George Shearing was once in a clumsy interview in which the interviewer tried to turn the discussion from Shearing's music to his blindness. "Have you been blind your whole life?" he asked. "Not yet," Shearing answered. After an awkward pause, the interviewer got back on track.

When prejudice and insensitivity cross the line into outright harassment, stronger responses are sometimes justified. Women who get obscene phone calls, or catcalls in the street, for example, may respond with something clever which puts the offender off balance. To the line "Hey, baby, I'd like to take your panties off," one woman answered, "I didn't realize you were wearing my panties!" Or the response may turn the offender's aggression back on him, to stop him in his tracks and take away his control of the situation. If you're walking down the street and a construction worker shouts, "Hey, baby, I want to get into your pants," Regina Barreca recommends shouting back, "Nah, I got one asshole in there already."[7] His co-workers will give him a hard time all day, and every man in the group will think twice before shouting anything at women again.

Now a response like that certainly violates the traditional rules for "lady-like" behavior. But to be "lady like" in this situation would be to silently tolerate the verbal attack, and that leaves the offender in control of the situation, encouraging him to abuse other women in the future. It's precisely because abuse like this has traditionally had no repercussions for its perpetrators, that it has continued for so long.

Women's humor, then, can be positive not only by supporting what's right in other people, but also by correcting what's wrong.

Sarcasm vs. Kidding

From our examination of negative and positive humor, we have seen that the best humor gives everyone a lift, rather than making some people feel good at the expense of others.

In building teams and good morale in the workplace, we simply cannot afford humor that divides and humiliates people. Racist and sexist humor are out, obviously, but so is most sarcasm.

"Sarcasm" comes from a Greek word meaning "to tear flesh with the teeth." Now some bosses enjoy putting people down as much as dogs enjoy tearing meat off bones, but their momentary pleasure seems to be the only possible benefit. Think of the last time you got sarcastic with your subordinates. Who was better off for the experience? You may have felt clever for a moment, but the people on the receiving end of your wisecracks felt humiliated and rejected for much longer.

Personal feelings are not all that get hurt by sarcasm. Enthusiasm, morale, and productivity depend on how people feel about themselves and their work, and having the boss humiliate them is one of the surest ways to make them feel lousy about both. Workers who are routinely put down don't feel part of a team, and, for fear of being ridiculed, are reluctant to take risks or even report mistakes.

In opposing sarcasm, I am not condemning good-natured kidding. Both sarcasm and kidding focus on people's mistakes and problems, but the attitude is different. In kidding people, we are not rejecting them or singling out their shortcomings as unique. Quite the opposite, kidding is accepting and universalizing—it focuses on what *one* of us did as something *any* of us might do. That's why in kidding sessions we often turn from what just happened to you, to stories about similiar problems we all face. This week it's funny that Ted got caught sneaking out of the meeting, but it's funny in the same way it was funny last week when I got caught doing the same thing, and it will be funny when the next one of us gets caught. That shows that what we are laughing at is not one person's problems, but rather the problems we share. People in dangerous work like mining, indeed, kid each other more than most co-workers, just because they have bigger problems to cope with together.

Unlike sarcasm, kidding people doesn't exclude them from our circle, but draws the circle around them *and* the rest of us, strengthening our bonds with them. We don't kid enemies or even strangers, precisely because we do not include them in our circle.

If for a month no one at work kidded you about anything, you'd start to wonder what was wrong. We value being kidded because it puts our individual situations in perspective and provides support. It reassures us that our problems are not unique, and that we can get by with a little help from our friends.

In-Group Humor vs. Negative Humor

Most of the examples of negative and positive humor discussed so far have been pretty clear-cut. Using racist or sexist humor to humiliate someone, for instance, would always be negative and wrong. But some humor which is positive for the group creating it—usually members of a profession—would seem negative to people outside that group. Indeed, such humor is usually carefully kept within the group to prevent it from offending outsiders.

I call humor intended only for inside a group "in-group humor," and we need to distinguish it from negative humor. Some of the best examples of in-group humor come from medicine. Nurses and doctors cope with life-and-death situations which could easily overcome them if they didn't have ways of blocking disgust, panic, sadness, and other negative emotions. As Vera Robinson reminded us in Chapter 5, medicine is a world of "illness, naked bodies, blood, guts, excrement, trauma and death."[8] Finding humor in what would otherwise be overwhelming is one way medical professionals keep their cool and so are able to do their work. But a lot of medical humor would disturb people outside the profession, especially patients and their families.

An example of what can happen when in-group humor leaks out to patients was reported in the newspaper a few years ago under the heading, "Pair sues hospital for calling child 'Smurfette.'" A pregnant woman had been injected with a blue dye to test for a urinary tract infection twelve hours before she went into labor, and her daughter was born blue. The medical staff, knowing that the coloring was temporary and harmless, nicknamed her "Smurfette," after the elfin blue-skinned cartoon character. As in-group humor, this nickname was positive, to raise their spirits and perhaps to distinguish the infant from a "blue baby," one born oxygen-deprived. But someone let the new mother hear the nickname, and that, as her lawsuit said, was "callous and distressing." The lesson here is obvious: in-group humor needs to be kept inside the group.

In one of my seminars for a convention of nurses, I used the exercise "Laughter or Tears" from the end of Chapter 2. The instructions are to take some funny story from work and retell it so that it sounds upsetting. One participant retold her story as follows:

> I was working in the psychiatric wing of the hospital on the sixth floor. One male patient was severely depressed and attempted suicide by jumping out a window. We rescued him before he got out the window.

Then, of course, the whole group had to hear how this story is usually told:

The man weighed 580 pounds and was dressed only in a hospital gown, which because of his size could not be tied at the back. The window he chose was only 20 inches wide, and so only his head and right shoulder fit into the opening. He got stuck. We found out he was in trouble when on the fifth floor we heard a voice from outside crying, "Help, help." We ran upstairs and into his room, and were faced with his gigantic backside sticking out at us.

Now as they were freeing the man from the window and taking care of him, it would have been inappropriate to laugh. But later on in the staff lounge, laughing about the event was a healthy way to bounce back.

Sometimes humor is internal to a particular group within a professional community. In one hospital department the nurses worked out a signaling system to let each other know which physicians were hard to deal with on any particular day. In their bathroom they had plastic chips with the doctors' names on them. The chips representing doctors who were being reasonable were on the back of the toilet on a satin pillow. The chips for the doctors who got only a "fair" rating for their treatment of nurses were placed on the edge of the toilet. And, as you might have guessed, the chips for the doctors who were being imperious and unreasonable were floating. The physicians weren't supposed to find out about this system, but when they did, there were unexpected benefits. Several were eager to know where their chip was each day, and they began to treat the nurses better.

Notes

[1] Thomas Hobbes, *Leviathan,* in John Morreall, ed. *The Philosophy of Laughter and Humor* (Albany: State University of New York Press, 1987), p. 19.

[2] Malcolm Kushner, *Lighten Up: How to Use Humor for Business Success* (New York: Simon and Schuster, 1990), p. 205.

[3] See Deborah Tannen, *You Just Don't Understand: Women and Men in Conversation* (New York: Morrow, 1990).

[4] Regina Barreca, *They Used to Call Me Snow White . . . But I Drifted: Women's Strategic Use of Humor* (New York: Viking, 1991), p. 116.

[5] Ibid., p. 197.

[6] Esther Blumenfeld and Lynne Alpern, *Humor at Work* (Atlanta: Peachtree, 1994), pp. 134-135.

[7] Regina Barreca, *They Used to Call Me Snow White . . . But I Drifted: Women's Strategic Use of Humor* (New York: Viking, 1991), p. 98.

[8] Vera Robinson, *Humor in the Health Professions,* 2nd ed. (Thorofare, NJ: Slack, 1991), p. xix.

CHAPTER 10

HOW'S YOUR LAUGH LIFE?

The Incongruity Theory Again

W
e'll wrap up by looking back over what
we've learned about humor and suggesting
some ways to incorporate more of it into
our lives.

In Chapter 2 we saw that humor is enjoying incongruity, that is, enjoying a clash between what we expect and
what we experience. Now in some simple traditional
cultures, where most people have the same beliefs and
attitudes, and life goes smoothly according to age-old
patterns, there may not be much incongruity and so not
much room for humor. Similarly, if we could set up a
utopia where everything went according to plan, there
would be little humor there. But in our complex, rapidly
changing society, where different people's ideas clash and
things seldom go strictly according to plan, incongruities
are all around us.

Not only is there a lot of room for humor today, but
having a sense of humor seems necessary to survive, or
at least to prosper. We simply can't function if we get
upset by everything that doesn't match our expectations.

Among the incongruities we experience, some are mild and easy to laugh at. In 1993 the Internal Revenue Service offered for sale gold-plated Christmas tree ornaments inscribed with the words "Many Happy Returns 1913–1993—Eighty Years of Income Tax." The goofiness of this gesture made a lot of people laugh. As Erma Bombeck commented, hanging an ornament on your Christmas tree as a reminder of your taxes is like making a paperweight out of your gallstones, or pressing a dirty diaper in your kid's baby book.

Most of the incongruities in our lives aren't as gentle as this, however. Many are big mistakes, failures, and misfortunes. Yet even with them there is room for humor. Indeed, seeing the humor in life's big incongruities is often the best way to survive them. The philosopher Frederick Nietzsche suggested that humans *had* to invent laughter because they suffered so much.

Erma Bombeck, as her readers know, found humor not just in trivia like the Income Tax ornament, but in the most serious problems. Her book *I Want to Grow Hair, I Want to Grow Up, I Want to Go to Boise*, for example, is about kids with cancer. To add to the incongruity here, after writing the book, Bombeck was herself diagnosed with breast cancer, which required a mastectomy. How did she react to the diagnosis?

> The humor that has been such an important part of my life kicked in automatically. I thought of the thousands of luncheons and dinners I had attended where they slapped a name tag on my left bosom. I always smiled and said "Now, what shall we name the other one?" That would no longer be a problem.

Nor did I give a thought to dying. I subscribe
to George Burns's philosophy, "I can't die yet.
I'm booked."[1]

Jokes like this about death remind us that not only are
there incongruities *in* life, but life itself, set against death,
is incongruous. The ultimate mismatch, as Stephen
Leacock put it, is "between the eager fret of our life and
its final nothingness."[2] And here, as with the smaller
incongruities within life, humor helps us cope. That's
why wise people from Socrates on have joked about
dying. On his deathbed Oscar Wilde looked around the
room and said, "This wallpaper is terrible. One of us has
to go." Some have even planned humor to outlast themselves. A tombstone in New Orleans reads "This is what I
expected, but not so soon." Dorothy Parker's says simply
"Excuse My Dust."

Look at the Big Picture

How is it possible to find humor in such huge incongruities as your own death? As we saw in Chapter 2,
what makes the difference between laughing and crying
is mental distance, stepping back from the incongruity to
see it in the big picture. To laugh at my own death, say, I
have to transcend my personal point of view to see
things more objectively.

If I think of my death only from my own perspective,
it looks like the end of the world. Indeed, it is the end of
my world. But in relation to the universe, or even the
history of life on earth, it's no big deal. All living things
die and make room for other living things. Hundreds of
thousands of people die every day, and one of these
days, like everyone before me and after me, I will be
among them.

At times we may wish that our lives went on forever, but think of how tedious and boring that would get. Can you imagine yourself at, say, your 2,528,409th birthday party? As Bertrand Russell said, most people who long for immortality don't even know what to do with themselves on a rainy afternoon.

In looking at ourselves objectively, we're no longer the center of the universe, and it's easier to see the humor in our life and even our death. Indeed in the big picture, the whole history of the human race can look funny. The more cosmic one's view of life is, the more comic it is. If there's a superintelligent race on some planet that has been watching activities on Earth for the last thousand years, by now they must watch us the way we watch reruns of *Gilligan's Island*.

Once we start looking at the big picture, too, we see that nothing is important all by itself, and nothing is important to everyone. Something is important only to someone with certain interests and goals. What is important to me today might be important to no one else, and next week it may not even be important to me.

What counts as a problem is also relative to our interests and goals. Having to build a wood fire to cook your dinner would be a big inconvenience in your home, but on a camping trip it's fun. The size of problems is relative, too; what counts as a big problem depends on what else has been bothering you. People who suddenly recover from terminal illnesses sometimes say that whatever other problems they had are no longer worth mentioning.

Here's an example, in a letter written by a college student to her parents, of the relativity of problems.

Dear Mom and Dad,

I'm sorry for not writing sooner, but hope you'll understand. First, sit down before you read further.

I'm doing much better now after recovering from the concussion I received from jumping out my dorm window in the fire last month. I can almost see normally thanks to the loving care of Norman, the janitor who pulled me from the flames. He more than saved me; he's become my whole life. I have been living with him since the fire, and we are planning to get married before my pregnancy shows.

Yes, I'm pregnant. I knew you'd be excited for me, knowing how much you wanted to be grandparents. We'd be married by now if it weren't for Norman's infection that prevented him from passing the blood test. I caught it from him, but the doctors are positive it won't affect the child.

Although Norm's not well educated, I know that you'll come to accept him as one of our family.

Your loving daughter,

Becky

P.S. There was no fire. I have no concussion. I'm not pregnant. There is no Norman. But I am getting an F in Biology, and wanted you to see that grade in proper perspective.

In many of our workplaces today, unfortunately, the accelerating rate of change and the large number of crises tend to push us into an alarm mode in which all problems look equally demanding of our attention. But approaching all problems full steam at the same time is a sure-fire way to burn out quickly. In order to survive and to get anything accomplished, we need to sort out the big deals from the small.

To keep my own sense of perspective, I have a plaque on the wall next to my desk. It reads:

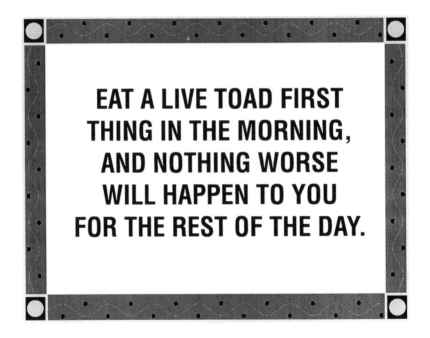

**EAT A LIVE TOAD FIRST
THING IN THE MORNING,
AND NOTHING WORSE
WILL HAPPEN TO YOU
FOR THE REST OF THE DAY.**

WHAT'S IMPORTANT?

Exercise 10-1

1. For each of the following events, describe a situation in which it would be fairly important, and a situation in which it would be fairly unimportant.

> A. You spill ketchup on your shoes.
> B. You lose your voice.
> C. Your house is blown away in a tornado.

2. Think of something you consider an urgent problem. Now imagine that you have just won the lottery for $10 million. What does that problem look like now?

3. Think of something you've wanted to do for a long time: learn to scuba dive, visit a friend in Alaska, or whatever. Now suppose that your doctor just told you that you have three months to live. What would you do?

4. To reconsider a scenario from Chapter 4, suppose that tomorrow morning's newpaper announces that a large comet is going to hit earth in one week, ending all life on our planet. What does the broken office copier or your spouse's annoying habit of leaving hair on the sink look like now?

5. What do your answers to these hypothetical questions reveal about how you should be living *right now in the real world*?

Don't Fret over Things You Can't Change

Besides looking at the big picture, we need to distinguish the things we can change from those we can't. A lot of useless worrying, unfortunately, focuses on situations that we can't do anything about. Stress, as we have seen, is composed of two emotions—fear and anger, and these evolved as ways of energizing animals to fight or flee when they were in danger. Today we feel the same kind of fear and anger early humans felt, but often we feel them in reaction to problems that won't be solved by fighting, fleeing, or anything else we might do. Anger and fear are useful emotions when you run into a mountain lion, say: they concentrate your mental energy on overcoming the danger, and they energize you to do just that. But in situations where nothing you can do will make a difference, getting scared or angry is wasted emotion. Worse, it sets you up for ulcers, heart attacks, and cancer.

If you've just sat down to a picnic on the grass and a thunderstorm comes up, all the anger you can muster will not reduce the rainfall by one drop. Make a joke about the storm, repack your basket, and head for cover. In life generally, when you face a problem, ask yourself if you can make a difference. If you can't, it's best to take a disengaged attitude. Look for the irony, folly, or absurdity in the problem, laugh at it, and get on with your life. The surest recipe for stress and depression is to go through life fully engaged with every problem we run across.

Play More

Humor, as we saw in Chapter 1, is a kind of play, and to cultivate our sense of humor it's helpful to cultivate our playfulness generally. When we play we are doing something because we want to, not because we have to. We play for its own sake, not to reach some further goal. Play is defined not by any particular activity, but by our attitude toward whatever we are doing. What is drudgery for some people, weeding a garden or making bowls on a potter's wheel, can be sheer pleasure for others.

Unfortunately, many of us do almost nothing for the sheer pleasure of it. Instead we spend virtually all our time on *tasks* that must be done to achieve goals. We get out of bed in the morning reaching for our "Things to Do" pad, and by the time we have ticked off the last thing, we are climbing back into bed. Life becomes, as the old saying goes, one damned thing after another.

In the task mode, pre-determined goals control our activity. In the play mode, on the other hand, *we* are the masters of our activity, and we can spontaneously re-structure the situation or go off in a different direction. In play we are freer, more flexible, and more self-directed than in the task mode.

Because a task demands certain results, too, it is future-oriented. If there is any satisfaction involved, it is later when, we hope, the goal will be reached. Play, by contrast, is oriented to the present: we get satisfaction from the activity itself at the moment we are engaged in it.

The extreme of the task-oriented person is the workaholic, who always needs to be striving for some goal. Even when they get a chance to play, workaholics often change what should be joyful activity into just another task.

"I play as hard as I work," an investment banker told me during a volleyball game in which his determination to win (he lost) kept him from enjoying what he was doing. I pointed out to him that he wasn't *playing* volleyball, any more than the men in the NFL *play* football. For him the game was another task, and since his team was unsuccessful at that task, he got no satisfaction from it. In an earlier conversation, he had complained that he found little zest in his life. After watching him in the game, the reason was painfully clear. He did nothing just for the fun of it.

Workaholics don't hurt just themselves, their families, and their friends by their joyless addiction to checking the next task off their list. In the long run, they hurt the organizations to which they are so committed. By not taking time for refreshment and play, they get stale, lose perspective, and set themselves up for stress-induced illnesses. The 10,000 Japanese businessmen who die each year of *karoshi* (overwork) certainly haven't done their former employers any favor.

Even though workaholics spend more time working than their peers who take time to play, studies show that they do not get significantly more accomplished. And because they are always in the task mode, they are not as imaginative or innovative. Dick Munro, former co-chairman of Time-Warner, is one business leader who declares himself "dead set against workaholics. Working like that causes you to lose enthusiasm and vitality and inhibits creativity." Munro says that throughout his long career at *Time* he very rarely took a train home later than 6 P.M.[3]

People often ask me about their boss or their spouse who "has no sense of humor." My answer is that there's no such thing as a normal adult without a sense of humor. As children we all had the ability to think and the ability to play, and humor is just a combination of these: it's thinking playfully. Your bosses or spouses, I point out, played and laughed as children. But after developing their sense of humor to a certain degree, they suppressed it by suppressing their playfulness. They probably adopted a very practical attitude toward life and accepted the Philosophy of the Third Little Pig that "Work and play don't mix." They didn't suppress their ability to think, however, and so all they need to unlock their sense of humor is to stop suppressing their playfulness. As Harvey Mindess says, you don't have to teach people to be funny. You only have to give them permission.

How can we become more playful? A good start is to consult the masters of play—young children. If you have kids, play with them and pay attention to how they play. If you don't have kids, borrow some.

Since my son was in preschool I have taken a morning off once a month to sit in on his class or accompany the children on field trips.

They're refreshingly different from adults. They ask lots of questions, say what they think, and are always on the lookout for new experiences. But perhaps the biggest difference is that most of what they do is done for its own sake. No wonder their laughter flows so easily.

Another way to become more playful is to visit a toy store regularly, preferably with a young child. Toys R Us and the other toy superstores are full of neat stuff. As the psychologist Paul McGhee suggests, being more physically playful will make you more mentally playful.

You might also spend an evening or two going through the book *Totally Useless Skills* by Rick Davis.[4] You'll learn how to make a clarinet out of a drinking straw, balance a feather on your finger tip, juggle scarves, hang a spoon from your nose, cut a hole in a business card big enough to put your head through, and dozens of other tricks. With a little imagination, you might even work some of them into your next presentation at work. Davis' book also contains the longest word in the English language—

PNEUMONOULTRAMICROSCOPICSILICOVOLCANOCONIOSIS

(a disease caused by a rupture of the lung that miners get when they breathe particles of sand as they dig through igneous rock). Memorize this word, and work it into your next conversation.

A big part of children's playfulness lies in their curiosity and desire to try new things. We can recapture some of the playfulness we had as kids by adding variety and novelty to our lives. At least once each day, break a habit.

- Brush your teeth or comb your hair using the other hand.

- Go to work a different way—walk, ride a bike, take the bus. If you have to drive, take a different route, and instead of parking close, to minimize walking distance and the number of people you run into, park far out in the lot to maximize both.

- At work say hello to someone you've never talked to. Have lunch with someone different.

- When you get home, do something unfamiliar. If you always have a beer, have a tall lemonade instead. Prepare something different for dinner—maybe that Thai recipe you saw in the newspaper last week.

- Switch roles around the house. If you usually empty the garbage and someone else does the dishes, trade jobs.

- Instead of watching the evening news on TV, listen to it on radio—on short wave radio from another country, if possible.

- When you read the newpaper, look at some section that you usually skip. Check the "Miscellaneous" or "General Merchandise" want ads. Think of what you could do combining the first three items listed. In my paper today, they are AIR PURIFIER, ARCADE GAME, and BATH TUB.

- Visit the public library and ask for copies of *LIFE* magazine from forty years ago. While you're there, pull down an encyclopedia and find a strange fact. Did you know that you have 62,000 miles of blood vessels in your body?

- Go to a Jaguar or Ferrari dealership and test drive the fastest car they have.

- If you're at all musical, buy an electronic keyboard (under $100) and learn to play it.

- If you travel for your vacations, this year try an unusual destination like St. John's, Newfoundland, or Reykjavik, Iceland.

Besides trying novel activities, be more experimental in familiar activities. Corporations today recognize the need to get more creativity from their people, and to do that, the progressive ones are trying to foster a supportive climate for risk-taking and making mistakes. The only people who take no risks and make no mistakes are those who aren't doing anything new, indeed who aren't making any real decisions. In the past such people may have been valued by authoritarian bosses, but today they are part of the problem rather than part of the solution. As Robert Kriegel reminds us, in the contemporary workplace the biggest risk is not taking any, and the biggest mistake is not making any.[5] Oscar Wilde applied this lesson to life as a whole: "Most people die of a sort of creeping common sense, and discover when it is too late that the only things one never regrets are one's mistakes."

A good example of the playful risk-taker is James Cannavino of IBM. Now a top executive, he began by walking into a branch office outside Chicago and talking his way into a job repairing keypunch machines. He got the position largely because he promised to work for six months without cashing his paychecks, until he had proven that he was the best keypunch repairer they had. That was his first risk at IBM—to support himself for those six months, he had to work nights in a pizza parlor. Years later as a computer engineer, Cannavino wanted to redesign a $6-million mainframe. Realizing that going through proper channels to secure one of the computers could take months, Cannavino instead made off with one. He visited the IBM manufacturing plant in Poughkeepsie, New York, where he found five of the mainframes bound for various locations. One wasn't needed right away, so he changed the shipping tag to route it to the laboratory where he worked. When it arrived, he and three colleagues began spending their evenings tearing it apart and improving its design. In three months, they had doubled its performance. Their design changes—now known as Virtual Machine Assists—became part of IBM's standard design and greatly boosted the company's competitiveness. What made it all happen was Cannavino's playful urge to hot-rod the machine, and his willingness to take risks to do it.[6]

The ideal is to become so playful in your work that the old line between work and play disappears. Instead of work being a necessary evil, and play what you might have a little time for after you get home, work and play will become one. The poet Robert Frost captured this ideal nicely:

> But yield who will to their separation,
> My object in living is to unite
> My avocation and my vocation
> As my two eyes make one in sight.
> Only where love and need are one,
> And the work is play for mortal stakes,
> Is the deed ever really done
> For Heaven and the future's sakes.

Keep Your Comic Eye Open

Several years ago this "Lost and Found" notice appeared in a newpaper:

> LOST DOG: 3 legs, blind in left eye, ear torn,
> recently castrated, answers to the name
> "Lucky."

Many people who spotted the notice made copies for bulletin boards, and within a month copies of copies were

259

appearing all over the country. It's now a classic piece of what anthropologists call "Xeroxlore."

What was so appealing about this little notice? Obviously, there's humor in the clash between the dog's name and his hard life. But there's deeper humor here. The notice captures not just the situation of that poor lost dog, but the bittersweet absurdity of our own lives.

Like lots of people, I can identify with Lucky. I've survived cancer, a messy divorce, being fired, and in any given week I can add to the list. Yet because I can step back from "modern life" and view it from a distance, the whole panorama has a certain funky charm to it, and even the worst spots are funny.

We're considerably luckier than Lucky in this respect. Dogs are locked into their own current perspective of the world; they can't see their lives with any distance, and so can't laugh. Human life is bearable, even fun, just because we can get this distance. Mahatma Gandhi put it bluntly: "If I had no sense of humor, I should long ago have committed suicide."

Our sense of humor works like a third eye. Just as our second eye adds depth to a flat world, our comic eye adds another dimension to our experience.

Looking at life with a comic eye is like viewing Earth from space. We are not overly attached to things and events. When mistakes and misfortunes occur, we stay clearheaded and in control, instead of being blown away by feelings. Humor is a thinking response rather than an emotional response to life. As Horace Walpole said, the world is a comedy to those who think, a tragedy to those who feel.

To keep your comic eye healthy, practice distancing. When things look terrible, ask yourself, "What would this look like to a person from Tahiti, to the *Candid Camera* crew, to a Martian? How would Erma Bombeck have written about this, or how would Gary Larsen have made it into a *Far Side* cartoon?"

Even easier, use distance in time: What will all this look like next week, next year, in ten years? As we said in Chapter 2, when old friends reminisce, much of their heartiest laughter is about events that didn't seem funny at the time. Just as we now look at crises from ten years ago and laugh, we can laugh at today's crisis *today* if we see it from the perspective of ten years from now. So laugh early—ten years from now you might not even remember this crisis to laugh at it.

One of the first things I see every morning, on the bathroom mirror, is a little slip of paper that looks like this.

HAVE A DAY.

© RPG, Inc. Reprinted by permission of Recycled Paper Greetings, Inc.

I can't help finding a deep truth here. It's this. When we get up each morning, we don't have a good day ahead of us. We also don't have a bad day. What we have is a day. Of course, what happens to us has something to do with whether it's a good or a bad day, but just as important is *how we look* at what happens to us. To a large extent we *decide* whether our lives are meaningful, fun, and worth living. As Abraham Lincoln put it, "Most folks are about as happy as they make up their minds to be."

So keep your comic eye wide open, and as the bumper sticker says, enjoy your life—this is not a dress rehearsal.

Notes

[1] Erma Bombeck, "Me Have Cancer?" *Redbook*, October 1992.

[2] Stephen Leacock, *Humor and Humanity* (New York: Henry Holt, 1938), pp. 219-220.

[3] Robert Kriegel, *If it ain't broke . . . BREAK IT!*, (New York; Warner, 1991) pp. 263-264.

[4] Rick Davis, *Totally Useless Skills* (New York: Perigree, 1991).

[5] Robert Kriegel, *If it ain't broke . . . BREAK IT!* (New York: Warner, 1991), pp. 159, 198.

[6] *New York Times,* May 10, 1992, F7.

For Further Reading

Adler, Bill, ed. *The Kennedy Wit.* New York: Bantam, 1964.

Allen, Steve. *How to Be Funny.* New York: McGraw-Hill, 1988.

Axtell, Roger. *Do's and Taboos of Business Public Speaking: How to Get Those Butterflies Flying in Formation.* New York: Wiley, 1992.

Barreca, Regina. *They Used to Call Me Snow White . . . But I Drifted: Women's Strategic Use of Humor.* New York: Viking, 1991.

Basso, Bob, and Judi Klosek, *This Job Should Be Fun.* Holbrook MA: Bob Adams, 1991.

Blumenfeld, Esther, and Lynne Alpern. *The Smile Connection: How to Use Humor in Dealing with People.* New York: Prentice-Hall, 1986.

Blumenfeld, Esther, and Lynne Alpern. *Humor at Work.* Atlanta: Peachtree, 1994.

Byrne, Robert. *1,911 Best Things Anybody Ever Said.* New York: Fawcett Columbine, 1988.

Cousins, Norman. *Anatomy of an Illness as Perceived by the Patient.* New York: Norton, 1979.

Cousins, Norman. *Head First: The Biology of Hope.* New York: Dutton, 1989.

Davis, Rick. *Totally Useless Skills.* New York: Perigree, 1991.

deBono, Edward. *Serious Creativity.* New York: Harper Business, 1993).

Eliot, Robert S., and Dennis L Breo. *Is It Worth Dying For? How to Make Stress Work for You—Not against You.* New York: Bantam, 1984.

Fassel, Diane. *Working Ourselves to Death.* San Francisco: Harper, 1990.

Fry, William F., Jr. *Sweet Madness.* Palo Alto: Pacific Books, 1963.

Garland, Ron. *Making Work Fun.* San Diego: Shamrock, 1991.

Goldstein, Jeffrey, and Paul McGhee. *The Psychology of Humor.* New York: Academic Press, 1972.

Goman, Carol. *Creativity in Business: A Practical Guide for Creative Thinking.* Los Altos: Crisp, 1988.

Goodman, Joel. *Laffirmations: 1,001 Ways to Add Humor to Your Life and Work.* Deerfield Beach, FL: Health Communications, 1995.

Handley, Cathy. *Encyclopedia of Women's Wit, Anecdotes, and Stories.* Englewood Cliffs, NJ: Prentice-Hall, 1982.

Hoff, Ron. *I Can See You Naked: A Fearless Guide to Making Great Presentations.* Kansas City: Andrews and McMeel, 1988.

Humor: International Journal of Humor Research. Subscriptions available from Walter de Gruyter, Inc., 200 Sawmill Rd., Hawthorne, NY 10532.

Iapoce, Michael. *The Business Speaker's Humor Handbook.* New York: Wiley, 1988.

Janis, Irving L. *Groupthink.* Boston: Houghton Mifflin, 1972.

Kaufman, Gloria, and Mary Kay Blakely, editors. *Pulling Our Own Strings: Feminist Humor and Satire.* Bloomington: Indiana University Press, 1980.

Koestler, Arthur. *The Act of Creation.* London: Hutchinson, 1964.

Kriegel, Robert. *If it ain't broke . . . BREAK IT!* New York: Warner, 1991.

Kushner, Malcolm. *The Light Tough: How to Use Humor for Business Success.* New York: Simon and Schuster, 1990.

LaBier, Douglas. *Modern Madness: The Hidden Link Between Work and Emotional Conflict.* New York: Simon and Schuster, 1986.

Laughing Matters. A quarterly magazine edited by Dr. Joel Goodman of The Humor Project, 110 Spring Street, Saratoga Springs, NY 12866.

Leacock, Stephen. *Humor and Humanity.* New York: Henry Holt, 1938.

Levering, Robert, and Milton Moscowitz. *The Hundred Best Companies to Work for in America.* 2nd ed. New York: Doubleday, 1993.

London, Oscar. *Kill as Few Patients as Possible.* Berkeley, CA: Ten Speed Press, 1987.

Ludovici, Anthony. *The Secret of Laughter.* New York: Viking, 1933.

McCormack, Mark. *What They Don't Teach You at Harvard Business School.* New York: Bantam, 1984.

McGee-Cooper, Ann. *You Don't Have to Go Home from Work Exhausted.* Dallas: Bowen and Rogers, 1990.

McGhee, Paul. *Humor: Its Origin and Development.* San Francisco: Freeman, 1979.

McGhee, Paul E. *The Laughter Remedy: Health, Healing and the Amuse System.* Available from the author at 56 Beaver Dam Road, Randolph, NJ 07869.

Metcalf, C.W., and Roma Felible. *Lighten Up: Survival Skills for People Under Pressure.* Reading, MA: Addison-Wesley, 1992.

Michalko, Michael. *Thinkertoys: A Handbook of Business Creativity for the 90s.* Berkeley: Ten Speed Press, 1991.

Morreall, John, ed. *The Philosophy of Laughter and Humor.* Albany: State University of New York Press, 1987.

Morreall, John. *Taking Laughter Seriously.* Albany: State University of New York Press, 1983.

Nash, Bruce, and Allan Zullo. *The Misfortune 500.* New York: Pocket Books, 1988.

Paulson, Terry. *Making Humor Work: Take Your Job Seriously and Yourself Lightly.* Los Altos, CA: Crisp, 1989.

Paulson, Terry. *They Shoot Managers, Don't They? Managing Yourself and Leading Others in a Changing World.* Berkeley: Ten Speed Press, 1991.

Pelletier, Kenneth. *Longevity: Fulfilling Our Biological Potential.* New York: Dell, 1982.

Peter, Laurence, and Bill Dana. *The Laughter Prescription.* New York: Ballantine, 1982.

Peters, Thomas J., and Robert H. Waterman, *In Search of Excellence.* New York: Harper & Row, 1982.

Peters, Tom. *The Pursuit of WOW!* New York: Vintage, 1994.

Peters, Tom. *Thriving on Chaos.* New York: Alfred A. Knopf, 1988.

Robinson, Vera. *Humor and the Health Professions.* 2nd ed. Thorofare, NJ: Slack, 1991.

Ross, Bob. *Laugh, Lead, and Profit.* San Diego: Arrowhead, 1989.

Solomon, Muriel. *Working with Difficult People.* Englewood Cliffs, NJ: Prentice-Hall, 1990.

Tannen, Deborah. *You Just Don't Understand: Women and Men in Conversation.* New York: Morrow, 1990.

Thompson, Charles. *What a Great Idea: Key Steps Creative People Take.* New York: Harper Collins, 1992.

Townsend, Robert. *Further Up the Organization.* New York: Harper and Row, 1984.

Townsend, Robert. *Up the Organization.* New York: Knopf, 1970.

Vaillant, George. *Adaptation to Life.* Boston: Little Brown, 1977.

Vasey, George. *A Philosophy of Laughter and Smiling.* London: J. Burns, 1877.

von Oech, Roger. *A Kick in the Seat of the Pants: Using Your Explorer, Artist, Judge, and Warrior to Be More Creative.* New York: Harper and Row, 1986.

von Oech, Roger. *A Whack on the Side of the Head.* New York: Warner, 1990.

Williams, Redford, M.D. *The Trusting Heart: Great News About Type A Behavior.* New York: Times Books, 1989.

Wilson, Steve. *The Art of Mixing Work and Play.* Columbus, OH: Applied Humor Systems, 1992.

Winokur, Jon, editor. *The Portable Curmudgeon.* New York: New American Library, 1987.

Wooten, Patty, editor. *Heart, Humor & Healing.* Mt. Shasta, CA: Commune-A-Key, 1994.

Wuertzer, Patricia and Lucinda May. *Relax, Recover: Stress Management for Recovering People.* San Francisco: Hazelden, 1989.